Longman Books for Teachers

THE TEACHING OF PROBLEM-SOLVING

Ian Instone

The author

IAN INSTONE is Co-ordinator of Cross-curriculum Studies at Tong Upper School in Bradford.

ISBN 0 582 02815 9

First published 1988

© Longman Group UK Ltd

All rights reserved. This work is copyright but copies of individual lessons, initiative tests and other tests may be made without fee or prior permission provided that these copies are used solely within the institution for which they are purchased. For copying in any other circumstances prior written permission must be obtained from the publishers and a fee may be payable. No other part of this publication may be reproduced, stored in a retrieval system, or transmitted in any form or by any means – electronic, mechanical, photocopying or otherwise, without prior written permission of the publishers.

Set in 11 on 13 point Palacio.

Printed in Great Britain by Longman Group Resources Unit.

Contents

Acknowledgments	iv
Introduction	1

Part 1

Summary	3
Lesson 1: Introduction to the Course	6
Lesson 2: Creative Graphic Communication	11
Lesson 3: Basic Graphic Communication	13
Lesson 4: Simple Graphic Presentation Techniques	17
Lesson 5: Sequential and Intuitive Thinking	24
Instone's 6-Block Tower Problem	27
Lesson 6: Creative, Divergent and Lateral Thinking	36
Lesson 7: Creative and Lateral Thinking I	41
Lesson 8: Development of Intuitive and Empirical Thinking Skills	44
Lesson 9: Creative and Lateral Thinking II	47
Initiative Test 1	49
Initiative Test 2	51
Initiative Test 3	52
Initiative Test 4	54
Initiative Test 5	56
Initiative Test 6	58

Part II

Summary	61
How to Solve a Problem	62
Answers to Questions about Problem-Solving	63
Lesson 10: Formulating a Problem – Objectives	67
Lesson 11: Formulating a Problem – Obstacles	70
Lesson 12: Interpreting a Problem	73
Lesson 13: Investigation, Using Topic Webs	78
Lesson 14: Producing 'Courses of Action'	87
Lesson 15: The 'Decision-making' Process	92
Test 1: The Problem-solving Process I	95
Test 2: The Problem-solving Process II	99

Part III

Summary	103
How to Design Something	104
Notes on the Design Process	105
A Worked Example: The Egg-support Problem	111
Design and Problem Bank	135
Design Briefs	141

Bibliography	142

Acknowledgments

The initial idea for the production of a course which would develop the strength of students' thinking skills was that of the Headteacher of Airedale High School, Mr G. Wain, to whom I owe my greatest thanks for his help, encouragement, and for giving me the opportunity and responsibility of leading an excellent team of teachers.

Success in promoting the course within a school can be put down only to the enthusiasm, dedication and hard work of the team I led at Airedale High School, who were initially involved in the development of a problem-solving course which was suitable for 4th and 5th year students, and had the potential of being accepted as an examination subject. It was accepted by the CSE board, and also was granted recognition by the RSA Education for Capability scheme.

I am also in debt to the South-east Bradford TVEI Consortium, based at Tong School, funded by the MSC, for allowing me the time and the funds to continue with my work in this very important area.

My thanks also go to Mr S. Sears, the assistant TVEI Co-ordinator, for all his help and open-mindedness while working closely with me in the promotion and further development of thinking skills in this initiative.

Professor K. F. Jackson, Lecturer at Bulmershe College of Further Education, gave me the inspiration and basis for this book and has helped me on numerous occasions. The many works written by Edward de Bono have also helped me to formulate exercises which should in turn help other people to develop their own creative and problem-solving skills.

Finally, I would like to offer my gratitude to Mrs J. Magowan, the retired Assistant Deputy Headteacher from Airedale High School, for the many hours of work and suffering I have given her while correcting my mistakes.

Introduction

Without enthusiasm, dedication, confidence and belief in the importance of developing thinking as a life skill, one should not undertake the teaching of this fascinating area, as a half-hearted attempt will only lead to failure. Edward de Bono sums this up when he says,

> 'The teacher is in the position of a tennis, football or athletics coach. A coach in such a position must know what he is doing; he must be definite and positive.
>
> The teacher must have a very clear view of what he is doing and what he expects from the pupils because if they do not know what they are doing they quickly lose interest.
>
> There is no doubt that the lessons are more successful when the teacher wants to do them. If the teacher has been told to do them the lessons are half-hearted and feeble . . . Furthermore the teacher who is not really interested will drift further and further away from the lessons until the pupils have no idea what is happening. On the other hand a teacher who is interested will introduce whatever variety he wishes but will still stay close to the spirit of the lessons.'
>
> *Edward de Bono* (1975)

Almost all students, even those who are considered to be of low ability, are capable of extending and raising the standard of their achievements. Traditional examinations are inadequate measures of what a person is capable of achieving. The usual pattern of work does not always improve a pupil's motivation, because of the constraints built into the traditional examination system; for example, the need to memorise hundreds of facts, syllabus content, lack of time to exercise creative skills and co-operate with others in joint projects, etc.

We live in a rapidly changing society, so we need to equip ourselves with those techniques and qualities which will enable us to adapt successfully to the demands of change. It is necessary to provide ourselves with the knowledge that society is dependent on new products and technology and, by familiarising ourselves with the process of creation and the properties of man-made artifacts and systems, we are contributing significantly to our education. Both the government and the employers want people who can think for themselves and have the ability to use their own initiative.

When pupils leave school they will be faced with many difficult situations, with no one there to tell them what to do next, unlike their experiences in school when help and advice were always available. Therefore, before they leave school, pupils need to be given the experiences and the challenge of working on their own and developing their own ideas and independence.

Thinking is a skill which can and should be taught to the stage where the pupil can practise the skill independently. The brain has the ability to deal with both logical and imaginative thinking skills and in order to cope with everyday life a combination of these different thinking processes is essential, carefully intertwined to produce a successful, creative thinker.

Although both types of thinking are used in school, the opportunity for them to come together and the time to develop them is not catered for in the normal school timetable. This means that a pupil very rarely has the chance to practise this important skill, and, because it is a skill, it must be practised if there is to be any development.

The first part of this course teaches students a process which will help them to think for themselves. It starts by breaking down traditional teaching techniques and removing the constraints that traditional methods often produce. At first the pupils usually find this a little unsettling because they no longer have the familiar security offered by traditional methods.

Students may find difficulty in thinking for themselves because they are rarely asked to, or given the opportunity. This course provides a guide, and the freedom and time to help the student with this necessary life skill.

Many studies have been made of the way we think and the one chosen for the second part of this course is the method suggested by Professor K. F. Jackson in his book *The Art of Solving Problems* (1983).

The third part of this course is concerned with the design process. To design something is, after all, to solve a problem. Therefore, this area must be considered in conjunction with the problem-solving process.

The word 'design' tends to be associated only with Art and CDT subjects, whereas it should be concerned with the whole curriculum. This broader connection will be developed during this part of the course.

Once students are familiar with the areas of problem-solving and design, they will be ready to tackle anything, because they will be equipped with a system to help them to formulate problems, interpret situations, produce courses of action, evaluate and come to the best decision and finally implement their solution. If this means designing something to deal with a situation, the students are also able to tackle this area.

The final part of this course is given to putting all of these skills into practice and each student works on a project which he/she has chosen him/herself, preferably from a situation the student has recognised as being a problem.

Part I

SUMMARY

Each of the following lessons begins with a set of simplified notes to enable the teacher to make a quick survey of the equipment and information required for each lesson. These are followed by detailed instructions and information relating to each of the exercises.

A definite time limit cannot be specified for each lesson, but it is important that a teacher is familiar with the material so that he or she will be able to judge the best timing for the age or ability range involved. Depending on the competence of the students and the expertise of the teacher, Lessons 2, 3 and 4 on graphic communication can either be missed out or tackled at a later stage. I have included them early in the course because I have found that it helps the students to produce better sketches when they are trying to communicate their ideas and solutions to the problems which may need graphic as well as written explanations.

The exercise book that I have found to be the most suitable for this type of course, which includes both sketchwork and written material and quite often a combination of both, is an A4, 25 leaf book, with all pages 5mm squared.

The contents of Lesson 1 (page 6) should make the students aware of the restrictions in the way we think and realise that it is possible to develop skills in this area. It is also to encourage enquiry and make students aware of the subtle difference between problem-solving and design and also how they are closely linked. They should also understand the need to work hand-in-hand if the most appropriate results are to be accomplished.

Initiative Tests can be found at the end of this first section. They serve the purpose of giving the students practice in developing the use of the imagination, lateral and divergent thinking skills. The ability to explore situations which at first glance appear to have no solution, and the need to look for more than one solution and discover from personal experience that the first idea produced is not always the best one are very valuable lessons to learn. Certain pieces of information in this book have been aimed at the student, this enables direct photocopies to be made which can be used as handouts. The Initiative Tests along with their instructions is one example of this practice.

Some of the methods used in the first section may appear, at first glance, to be strange or even outrageous. This is intentional, because the need to allow creativity to develop requires creative as well as established approaches. One of the main causes of slow progress in certain areas is our natural tendency to reject anything which at first glance makes us feel uncomfortable without initially exploring all of its possibilities.

Marathon runners use various exercises and diets and train at different speeds, depending on the type of terrain or distance involved, to help them become suitably equipped to tackle the apparently more formal structure of the actual event. Like the athlete, I feel that it is also necessary to equip oneself with varied techniques in creative thinking, demonstrated in Part I, before moving on to the more formal structure of the problem-solving described in Part II.

All of the following lessons have been tried and tested on a very wide age range and I have found them all to be successful.

Aims

The aims of this course are:

1. To extend and exploit a creative imagination;
2. To develop a greater understanding and awareness of the variables involved in the terms 'problem-solving' and 'design', including their significance, meaning and usage;
3. To encourage skills, both practical and intellectual, in problem-solving and design, through a process of analysis, synthesis or realisation;
4. To develop co-operation, social responsibility, initiative and resourcefulness;
5. To extend a student's ability in communication skills;
6. To show that a wide range of knowledge across the whole curriculum is a main characteristic of problem-solving, involving large numbers of diverse considerations;
7. To make students aware that expression through the ability to draw, sketch and construct models, and to communicate ideas in speech and writing are an essential part of the process of problem-solving and designing (or even evaluating designs), and they assist one's judgment in making decisions.

Assessment Objectives

Students will be expected to demonstrate the ability to:

1. Formulate a problem giving a clear statement of both objectives and obstacles;
2. Interpret the situation through analysis and research, highlighting the main elements of the problem;
3. Produce courses of action to overcome the obstacles and reach the objectives;
4. Evaluate courses of action and make decisions;
5. Prepare a brief against which design proposals can be tested so as to overcome the difficulties identified;
6. Analyse, research and propose responses to the brief and to choose, and, where necessary, to justify, the most appropriate;
7. Develop or express this response and, wherever possible, to bring it to some practical conclusion;
8. Analyse and evaluate the result and communicate findings to others and show how decisions can be implemented;

9. Demonstrate, through this work, an understanding of the influence of aesthetic, social, cultural, environmental and technological considerations.

The pattern of the course and range of activities for each individual will vary according to the areas of knowledge explored. However, each individual will cover a regulated sequence of experiences as shown in 'How to solve a problem' (page 62) and, when applicable, 'How to design something' (page 104) which will be applied to particular examples.

Motivation is increased when a child is working on a problem which is relevant to him/herself. Therefore, whenever possible, pupils should be encouraged to work on their own problems and only work from the problem bank when they have difficulty finding their own problem situations (a problem in itself!).

LESSON 1: INTRODUCTION TO THE COURSE

Objective

To make a pupil aware that a problem may have many solutions and to promote the use of the imagination. Also to illustrate some conventional thoughts and their inhibitive nature.

Resources

Slides of da Vinci's design work
Set of unusual objects
Variety of chairs, e.g. deck chair, bean bag etc.
A4 drawing paper

Content

Show slides or pictures of da Vinci's work to the group and develop a discussion about the diversity of ideas on one theme.

Using the example of the designs for scaling ladders (see Teacher Notes below) ask the students to try to work out the original problem that da Vinci was trying to solve, which was to try to take over a castle or its contents or both. This could have been tackled in many other ways and should stimulate further discussion.

Ask the pupils to draw a chair, and highlight the similarity in sketches. Show how the majority of them have been influenced by the basic elements of a chair, then show or illustrate different types of seat. Develop ideas for further variations of seat.

Issue unusual objects to groups of pupils for their consideration and ask them to produce a list of suggestions about their original functions and also explore possibilities of giving them alternative uses. Later in the lesson these are shared with the other groups to demonstrate a wide variety of thoughts and ideas.

Assignment

Issue Initiative Test 1 (page 49).

Emphasise the need for diversity in possible solutions.

Teacher Notes

There is nothing new about design; it is a very old process and something we all have to do, probably many times each day – for example, when we have to remove the tightly stuck top of a bottle, or the top of a can without the conventional opener, or retrieve a small object from an inaccessible place. Another example of design can be taken from an uneducated labourer working on a building site who had not had any breakfast but had some raw bacon, an egg and a brazier full of hot coal. He cooked the bacon over the fire holding it with a piece of wire and dripped some of the released fat onto a clean shovel to fry the egg. He could also have fried the bacon on the shovel or used a stick instead of wire. All these examples of design could be interpreted as problem situations. In some cases the distinction between the two areas can be very small. Three of the above examples involved the problem of satisfying a requirement of thirst or hunger and in all of these cases the decision had been made to directly tackle them by designing or creating some form of aid. Finding alternative methods to satisfy the thirst or hunger would be problem-solving. In the example of retrieving the small object from an inaccessible place, once again the decision to acquire the item had already been made. Therefore, it is another design situation.

Animals, birds and insects also have the ability to design. For example: birds build nests, spiders make webs, bees create honeycombs and beavers erect dams. Humans, in fact, often copy the designs of other life forms. Nature tends to form its own patterns which usually have fairly strict guidelines. The webs of spiders can quite often be used to identify the type of spider, or the construction and size of nest to identify the bird. However, the positions of the webs, nests etc., can never be completely identical and obviously present slightly different problems for construction. This means problem-solving has to occur before the actual design, which may also vary, can be produced.

We, as humans with greater brain capacity and knowledge at our fingertips, can obviously produce far more varied designs than each of the lower life forms which tend to stick to the one successful pattern. However, can we compete with them in their ability to solve problems in their speciality areas? When a difficulty arises, they do not immediately give up, but try other courses of action, such as different materials for nests, alternative anchor points for webs, or, if an obstacle is in their path, they will tackle it in a variety of ways. This is because they have to if they want to survive. The more practice they have, the better they become at dealing with problems.

We rely heavily upon one another and most of the thinking and decision-making has been done for us by someone else. This means we do not bother, or rarely have the chance to think for ourselves, which in turn means that we do not practise this important skill. Consequently, when a problem does come along, we are unable to make a successful attempt at solving it and quite often make a wrong decision, or run to someone else for help.

Problem-solving and design are very closely linked; in fact, there are many people who would say that they mean the same thing. That is, to design something is to solve a problem. However, for the purpose of this course they are kept as two distinct units.

Let us look at some of the work produced by one of the great inventors who was prolific in ideas: Leonardo da Vinci. If you examine the pictures of his work they show a great variety of ideas but he appears to have worked mainly from a design brief, having first worked out in his head a solution to a problem. We do not see his original thinking of the various ways of tackling the problem, which is the area we are concerned with in the first two sections of this book. For example, if one examines a picture of his designs for scaling ladders, it shows a great variety of ideas for climbing a castle wall but does not explore all the other ways the original problem could have been solved. The problem in this case was finding a way to take over the castle or its contents. Just because you are good at designing scaling ladders does not automatically mean that you are pursuing the best way of entering a castle.

It is a useful exercise to imagine yourself with attachments that give you all the skills and powers of all other life forms and natural elements. By doing this it breaks down the in-built barriers in our brain which tend to cause us to dismiss, without any consideration or exploration, ideas which may appear silly or impossible. At first sight the ideas may not work but if they are given some thought they may with a little, or a lot of modification, produce alternative solutions, or even new or different designs. Until you have fully explored all the possible avenues and evaluated every one, you cannot justifiably set them aside.

Using the above example of scaling ladders, we should ask ourselves, 'What was the original problem?' The answer, of course, is to take over the castle, or contents, or both. Now imagine yourself with all the powers and skills mentioned earlier, including all the abilities of plants, animals, insects, birds, and the powers of nature. There is the cunning of the fox, the power of the charging rhino, the climbing skills of the insects, the explosive force of the volcano, the destructive force of fire, the stored energy in a dried seed pod with the ability to catapult its contents, the tunnelling power of the worm, the flight of the bird, butterfly, spider and seed etc.

Here are just a few alternative courses of action which could have been taken to gain entry into the castle:

Knock down the gate
Fire tear gas inside
Burn down the gate
Blow a hole in the wall
Tunnel under the wall
Climb the walls with suction pads
Vault over
Use trickery, for example, 'the wooden horse of Troy' technique
Catapult over
Fly over and parachute down to the ground

Nowadays, all of the above ideas are feasible, but in the earlier days of capturing castles some of the above ideas would have been dismissed as silly or impossible. The possibility of men flying and falling slowly down to earth, tear gas, or a substance that exploded with great force, would have been given little serious consideration.

As mentioned earlier, we still suffer from an unwillingness to think about concepts which at first glance appear unreasonable. It we learn from the above example, that by considering and exploring what at first appears impossible, we are given the opportunity to produce new ideas; concepts which, at the moment, are out of the question, or labelled as not worth considering, may be completely acceptable in the future. Any self-respecting designer, however, has always looked at the possibility of improvisation or circumvention of the problem before embarking on a new project.

The use of lateral and divergent thinking skills is very important in the development of our ability to discover or generate new ideas.

If a group of students is asked to sketch a chair very quickly, you will discover that they usually all tend to follow the same guidelines in their constructions, which is a standard framework chair with a seat, a back and four legs. We are so conditioned that the use of the word 'chair' has the effect of restricting our thinking. This effect of the terminology limiting our thought process will be considered in the design section later in this book. A chair is a seat which will support your weight and could have taken the form of a deck chair, a bean bag, a bale of straw, a block of shaped foam, an inflatable, a shooting stick, an easy chair, a stool etc. This simple exercise shows how difficult it is to escape from traditional thinking. If the terminology used in asking the students to sketch a chair had been changed to say, 'Sketch a device which would support the weight of a human in a sitting or reclining position', we would have had far more variation in the types of seat produced. This means we, as teachers, must choose our words carefully when asking pupils to produce work, otherwise we may restrict their creative ability. We must also encourage and teach students to formulate their own problems, to give them a clear view of what they are trying to achieve.

Another technique which can be used here, is to take the example of the chair once again and ask the students to draw a seat with three legs, e.g. a milking stool, then share all the various ideas amongst the group. Then ask the students to sketch a seat with two legs, e.g. a deck chair, a seat with two solid square blocks for legs, two vertical legs with horizontal rails across the bottom to give them stability, and so on. Follow this with ideas for seats with one leg, e.g. pouffe, bean bag, column or shaped block, etc. Finally, ask them to sketch ideas for seats with no legs, e.g. a seat attached to a wall, a swing suspended from the ceiling, an inflatable supported by water, a positive magnetic seat on a positive magnetic base which will suspend the seat, or air pressure suspending a hover-seat. It could be argued that some of the one-legged seats mentioned above have no legs or even lots of legs and that some of the no-legged seats do have legs, such as the wall or water counting as legs. If it does create discussion and creative thinking it has served its purpose well.

Design teams quite often set themselves problems or briefs to help them to keep their creative thinking skills alert. On one occasion such a team chose the theme of 'aeroplane'. From this they extracted the elements and then just concentrated on one of these: the seating. The unusual idea emerged of making the seating edible so that if the plane crashed in a remote area and they ran out of food they would have something to sustain them.

Continuing with the theme of creative thinking, divide the class into smaller groups of two to four and issue each of them with an unusual object. Each group of students tries to work out what the object was used for and then makes a list of alternative uses. After a few minutes the groups circulate the objects and repeat the process until each group has examined all of the objects. Unusual objects can be obtained from the Museum Service. They have groups of unusual items which are catalogued under the heading of ' "What is it?" boxes'. However, these are in great demand and need to be ordered well in advance. Another idea for materials is slides or photographs of articles. A further source of ideas can be obtained from a series of books produced by Shire Publications Ltd. I found *Shire Album 4, Old Farm Tools* by John Vince a very useful collection. As well as taking slides and photographs to show to the students, I also made models of the items, which alleviated the difficulty of borrowing objects.

When the groups have examined all the objects a class discussion should take place and the ideas shared amongst the students. An additional assignment, to be completed for homework, can be issued at the end of the lesson. Initiative Test 1 (page 49) is ideal at this stage, because it involves a problem which has many diverse solutions. Some possible courses of action follow the initiative test but I am sure you will be able to extend the list much further, thus demonstrating that we should not be content with our first ideas.

LESSON 2: CREATIVE GRAPHIC COMMUNICATION

Objective

To introduce the students to creative thinking expressed in the form of sketch work and presentation by the production of an appropriate and original design to apply to the front cover of each student's exercise book. The theme in this case is problem-solving.

Resources

A2 drawing paper
Examples of lettering
A wide selection of materials to stimulate ideas, e.g. magazines
Coloured foil
Clear self-adhesive plastic sheet
Various adhesive tape
Vivelle
Coloured card
Coloured paper
Various wallpapers
Scissors
Craft tools
Cutting boards
Various glues
Coloured pencils
Felt tips
String
Pencil spray guns
Coloured tissue
Compass
Stencils
Rulers
Letraset
Pencils
Rubbers

Content

Introduce the students to simple graphic design work related to the theme of problem-solving. Consider lettering, size, texture, background shape, background, materials, use of colour, tone etc.

Ask the students to sketch at least four totally different ideas which could be related to problem-solving. (Possibly make a list of areas which could be considered and ask students to explore them pictorially.)

The initial designs or ideas need only be in a rough but presentable sketch form. Each idea must be accompanied with a full explanation of the materials and processes which could be used – the size, what stimulated the idea, any other research information and a brief final evaluation.

Teacher Notes

A class discussion is essential to enable the students to share ideas about the theme of problem-solving. The resulting list of ideas for exploration should be copied by all students, to enable them to remember them when working on this assignment at home.

I have found that the students are usually quite creative about the term 'problem-solving', with ideas ranging from simply playing about with the lettering, to more creative ideas which suggest the theme. However, the rectangular shape of the front cover and any size restriction you may place on the final design, which would normally be given as a length and width measurement, tends to limit the ideas for the shape of the background to square and rectangular (if indeed a background is needed at all).

It is also useful to examine as many materials as possible and explore the properties of each and what processes can be performed on each of them, e.g. 3-D effect, embossing, piercing, texture, layering, combination of materials, etc.

At least four designs need to be produced for the following lesson and any special materials which the student needs to be incorporated in the final design, such as magazines, picture cards, etc., must be acquired by them and brought to the lesson.

It is important that from very early on in this course all students should have a basic understanding of simple, pictorial sketchwork, and the competence to apply shading to enhance and clarify their drawings. Communication of ideas does not only rely on the ability to write fluently, but also the skill to draw in a way which can be understood.

I have found that even though students have followed a basic Art course, most of them appear to be unable to transfer or use their skills in other areas and the following two lessons are to teach, or at least to remind them, of some sketchwork techniques. The ability to communicate information clearly, both in written and graphic form, is not only necessary to be able to deal with many of the later exercises, but a requirement of many other subject areas, whilst in school, and as an important skill all through life.

LESSON 3: BASIC GRAPHIC COMMUNICATION

Objective

To ensure that all of the students are capable of communicating their ideas in an acceptable pictorial form.

Resources

HB or B pencils
Exercise books

Content

Use the Teacher Notes below.

Check all of the students' work at each of the stages and if necessary give individual tuition.

The use of pencil rubbers should be discouraged and the correct use of the pencil encouraged: that is, light construction linework for the rough draft by holding the pencil away from the point and only using gentle pressure with confident strokes, and dark, thin linework for the finished lines by holding the pencil close to the point.

Develop confidence in the application of pencil strokes. Mistakes will occur frequently and are an accepted part of the process, providing they are contruction lines.

Assignment

Issue Initiative Test No. 2 (page 51).

Teacher Notes

I have found that a double period (1 hour 10 mins) is just long enough to spend on this lesson, unless the group is a large one, or of low ability.

The size and layout of the sketches in the exercise book should be discussed before starting. Also a demonstration of the different types of linework which are needed and how to produce them.

I recommend three sketches to a page and these should be large enough collectively to fill the page.

Discourage dividing the page into three: allow freedom in the positioning of each sketch.

Most of the students will lack confidence at this stage and this has the effect of them producing very small drawings with jerky linework. However, at the end of this short lesson I have always found that the majority of the students, if not all of them, have developed a style, understanding and confidence, which helps them considerably during this course.

As already said, discourage the use of pencil rubbers. They should not be needed, even if dozens of mistakes are made, because they all should be in faint construction linework. However, I recommend that you have a couple of good quality pencil rubbers tucked in your coat pocket for emergencies.

Rulers, or straight edges of any kind, are not allowed to be used.

Suggested Lesson

1. Ask the students to draw a freehand sketch of the three axes used in isometric projection.

   Pupils need to be able to visualise 30° and 90°.

   Students should practise drawing the construction lines several times, covering over each previous attempt, until a satisfactory straight line of the correct length and angle is produced. Once it looks correct, change the correct lines to finished lines, or dark thin lines. The construction lines should be faint enough to disappear into the background when the dark lines are added.

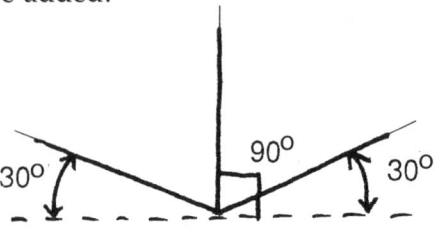

2. Ask the pupils to sketch a cube: size is important.

   First of all, draw the faint axes. Then step off the approximate sizes of width, length and height. Project lines at 30° and 90° from the appropriate points, in construction linework, then continue the drawing to produce a faint cube. This means that corrections can be made without having to rub it out.

   Now change the correct lines to dark ones. (All lines should be at 30° or 90° and parallel.)

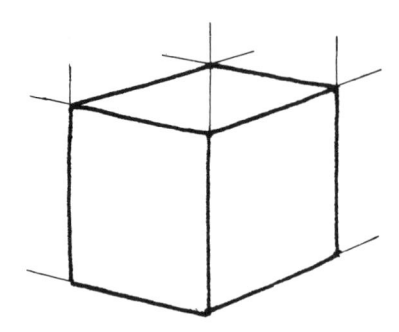

3. Use the same procedure as in No. 2 only this time construct a rectangular box.

4. Ask the students to draw another cube but this time only allow 45 seconds to complete it. The ability to put their ideas quickly down on paper must be developed.

5. Ask the students to draw a circular sectioned tube.

   First of all, in construction linework, sketch a tall rectangular box and imagine that it is transparent, so sketch in the back of the box as well.

Then estimate the centre of each of the four sides on the top and bottom of the box and mark with centre lines. Draw a construction line oval on the top and bottom of the box. The elipse should contact each of the four sides at the centre points which have been marked. (The major axis is horizontal to the paper.) The mistake that occurs most frequently at this stage is shortening in the length of the major axis of the elipse. Point this out to the students and encourage them to stretch the elipse well into the corners on the major axis. The vertical sides of the tube can now be constructed, then all of the correct lines can be changed to finished lines.

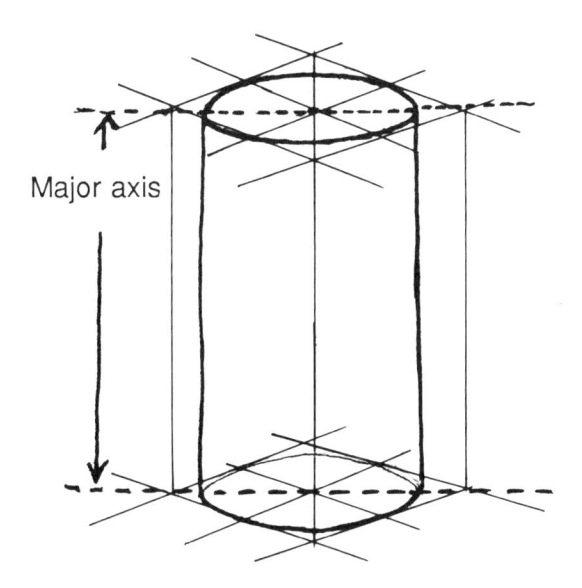

6. Use the same procedure as in No. 5, only this time draw a cone using a construction line cube to assist the drawing.

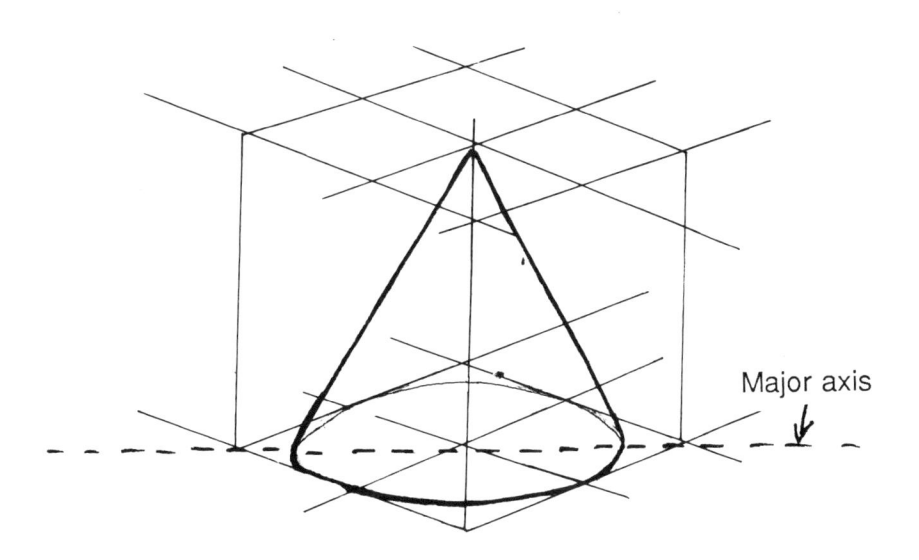

15

7. Imagine that a strip of card has been folded to form a letter 'W'. Draw it in isometric projection.

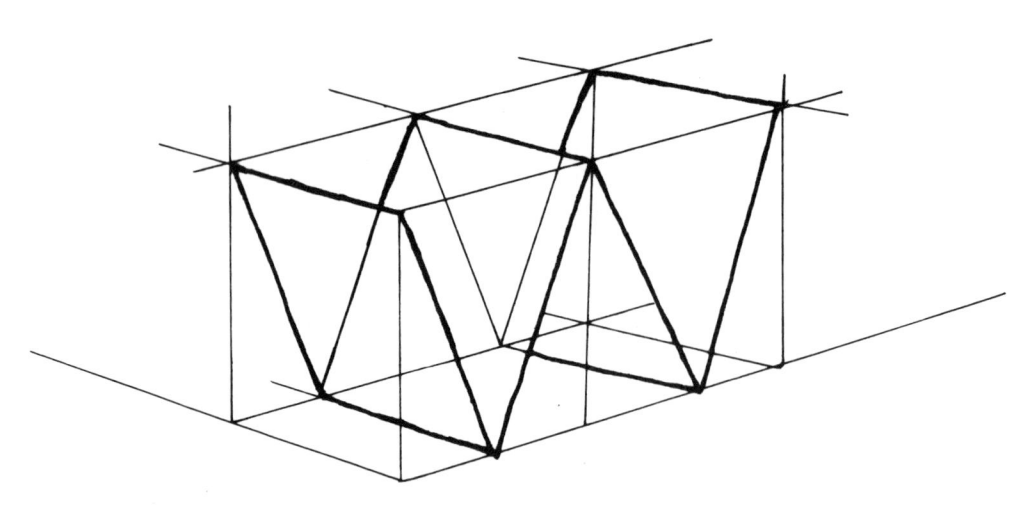

The students find it easier if they divide the rectangular box into two equal parts and then construct the two 'V' shapes which make up the letter 'W'. These can then be projected onto the back of the construction line box, followed by the insertion of the remaining connection lines. Finally, all of the correct lines can be converted into finished lines.

Constantly stress the need for light construction linework.

8. Construct a drawing, in isometric projection, of a letter 'X' which is made out of 25 mm wide strips of card.

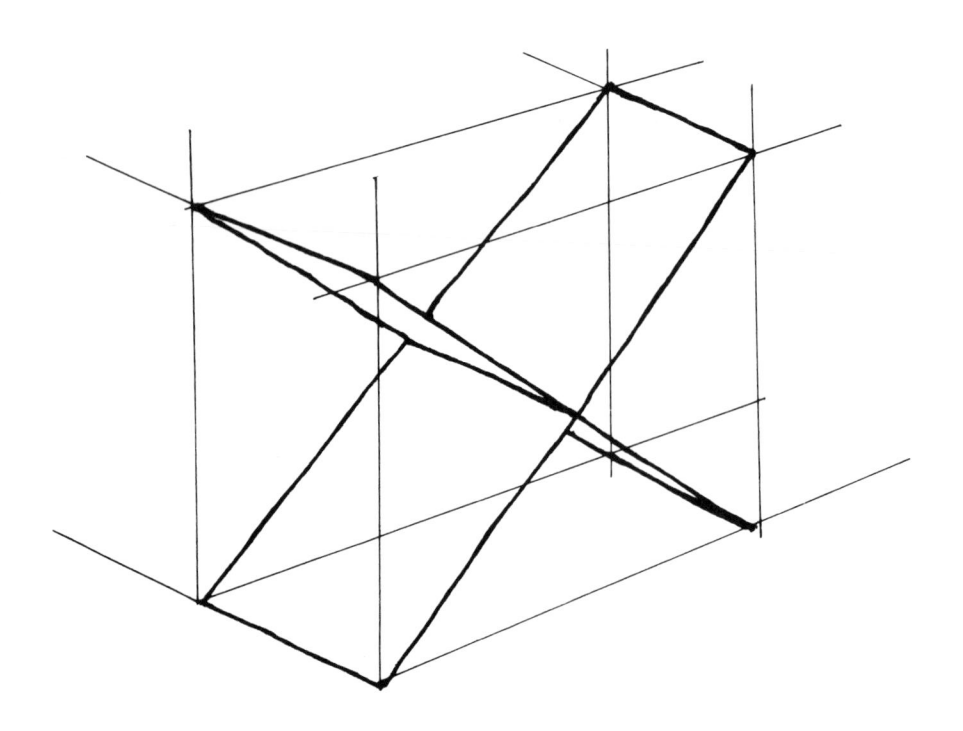

LESSON 4: SIMPLE GRAPHIC PRESENTATION TECHNIQUES

Objective

To enable students to enhance their pictorial work in such a way as to show an understanding of the effect of light and tone on various shaped objects.

Resources

A2 drawing paper
Watercolours
Water
Containers for paint and water
Selection of different sizes of artists' brushes
Felt-tip pens
Coloured pencils
Exercise books
Fine-tipped black felt-tip pens

Content

Using the drawing paper, demonstrate various methods of applying tone to sketches of cubes, cones, cylinders and spheres.

Ask the students to apply colour and tone to the orthographic sketches they produced on the previous lesson.

Unless the exercise books are made from a high quality paper, the use of watercolour and wide felt-tip pens is not advisable as they tend to soak through, distorting the paper and spoiling the following sheets.

Assignment

Select a simple object and sketch it. Then observe the light effects upon it and apply appropriate tones, using any medium of their choice provided the paper they use is of a high enough quality.

Teacher Notes

Examples of some of the demonstrations that I have used in the past are shown on the following pages.

In the original, this drawing showed how different tones of the same colour could be used to produce a 3-D effect. I also used a fine, black, nylon-tipped pen to edge the sketches because I like the effect that it produces. Shading around the outside of the object can be used to soften the effect of the dark edging.

It is important to note that a fairly wide felt-tip pen is needed to cover wide areas and also the direction of shading needs to be kept in the direction of the plane being shaded.

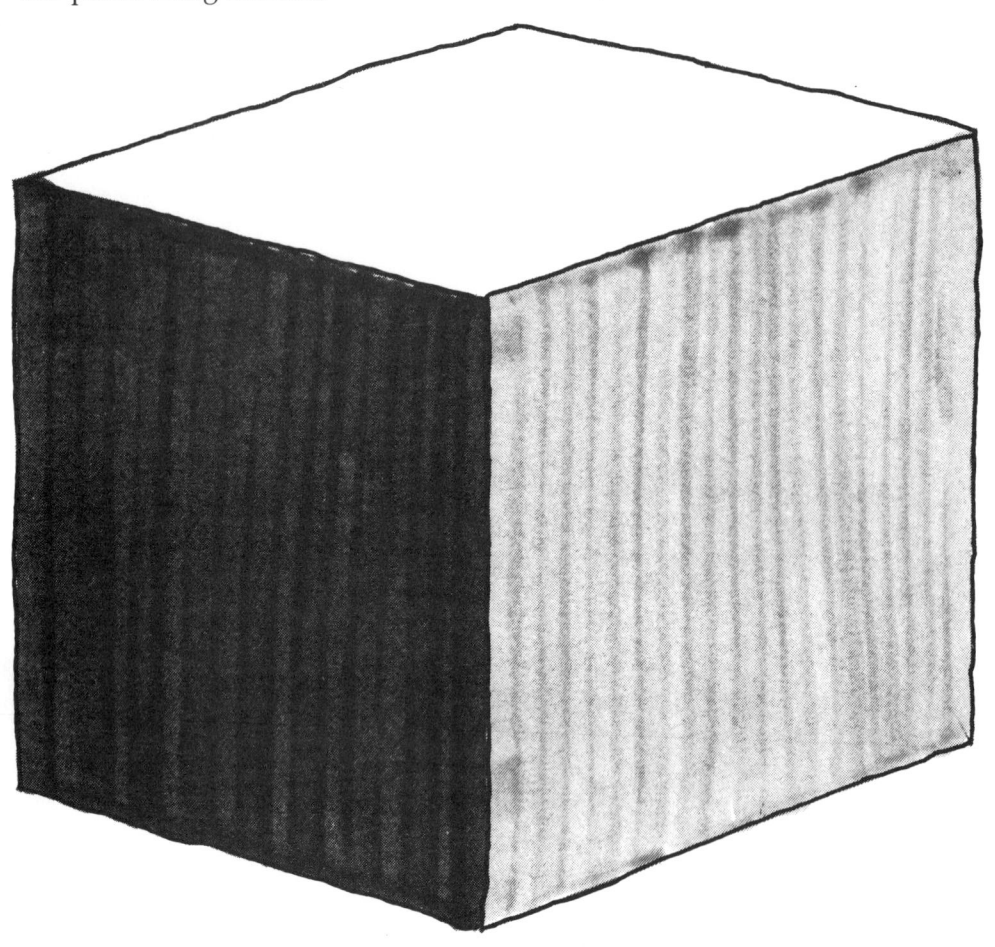

When different tones of the same colour are not available, it is possible to use the technique shown below. In the original sketch all the faces of the object which were not receiving direct light were shaded the same colour and tone; then on the face receiving the least amount of light, additional tone was added by applying a coating of grey. It is important to allow a certain amount of the base colour to show through the grey.

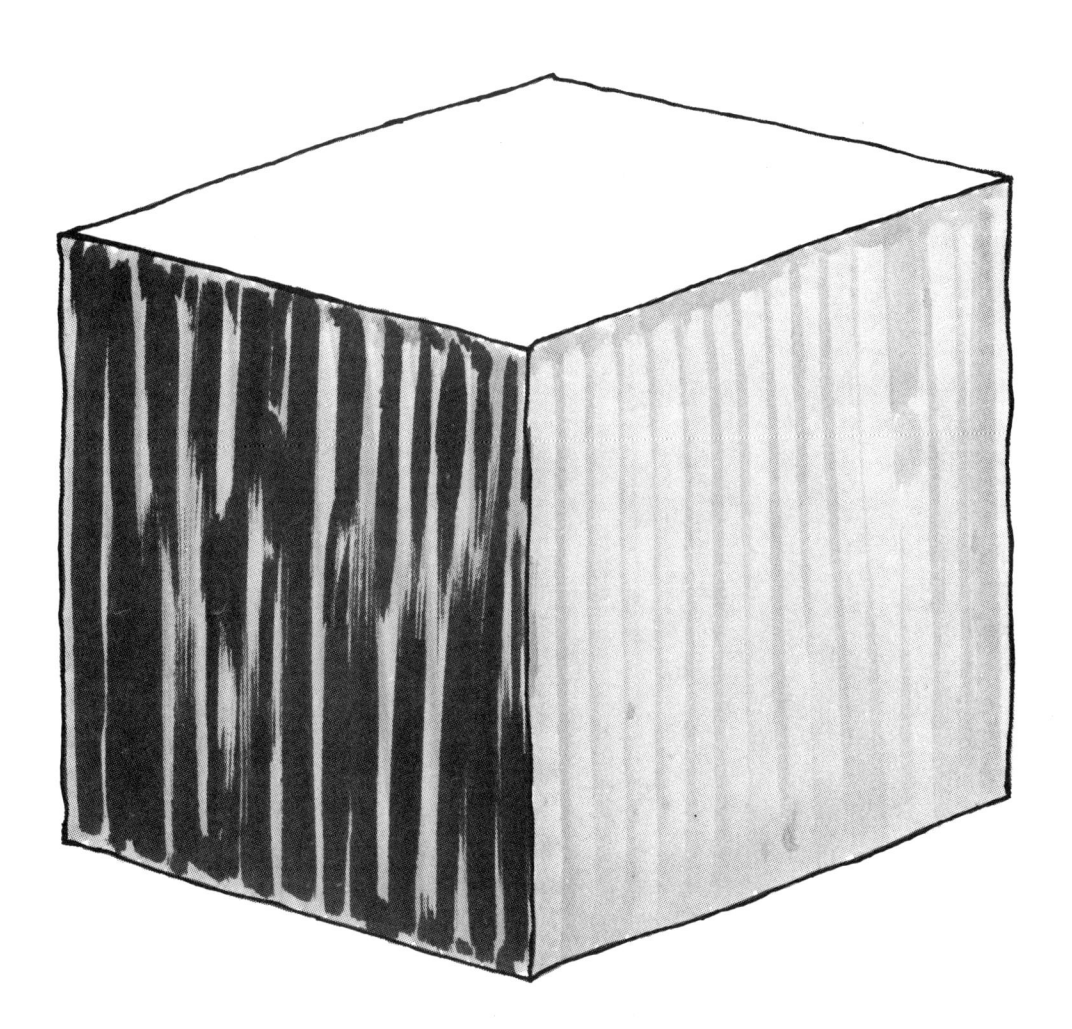

Quite a pleasing effect can be obtained by the addition of thin black lines which follow the directions of the planes. The closer the lines are placed together, the darker the surface appears. The advantage of using this effect is that various tones on one surface can more easily be obtained.

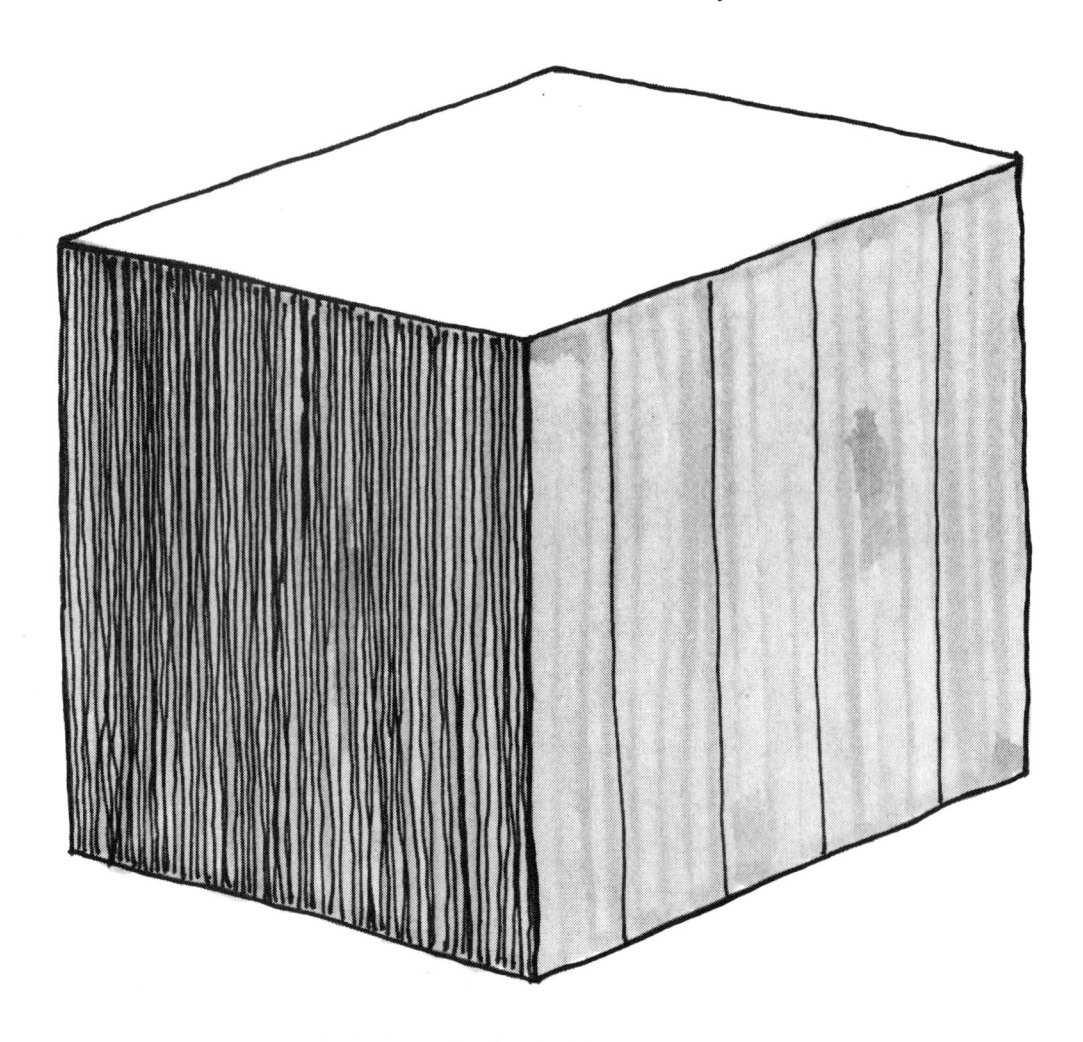

The following are examples of sketches which have been shaded only by the use of line.

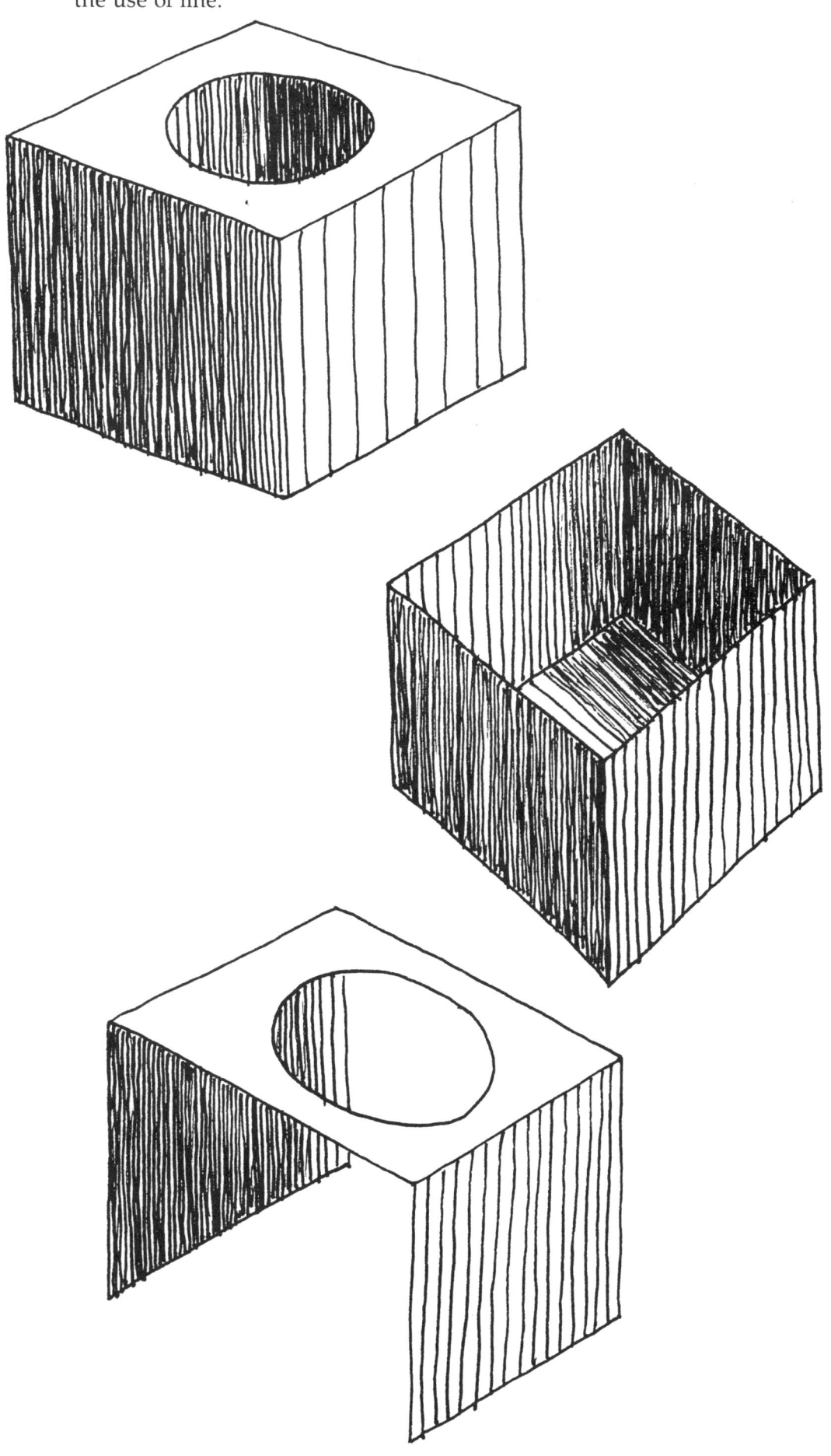

Here are various shaped objects shaded by the line technique.

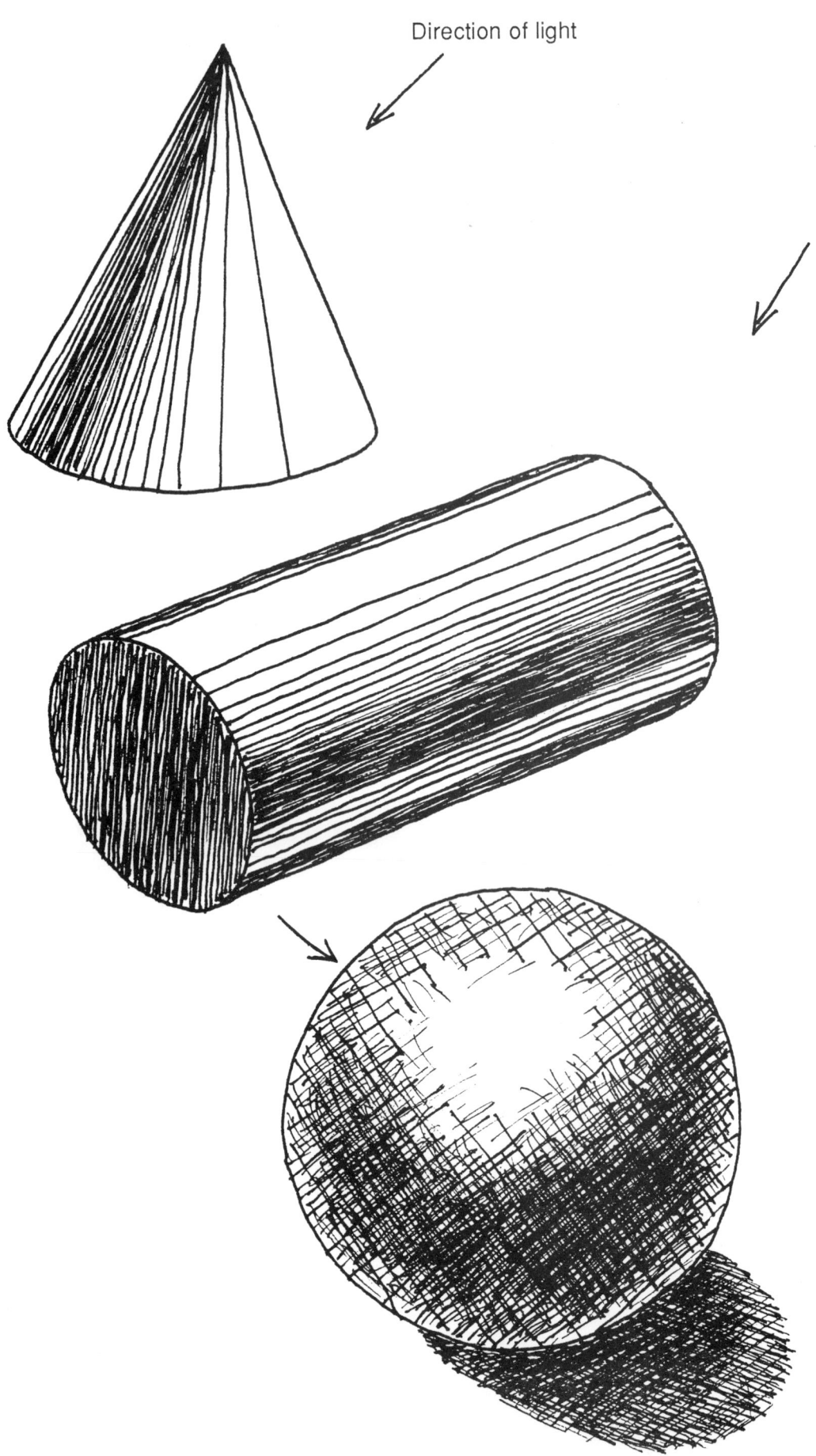

Direction of light

The sketch below shows one of the effects that I prefer to use. The original sketch is a combination of the use of coloured pencils, linework and background colour.

The introduction of perspective work can be made at this stage.

LESSON 5: SEQUENTIAL AND INTUITIVE THINKING

Objective

To encourage students, through the technique of trial and error (intuitive thinking) to produce more than one solution to a problem thus increasing their ability to overcome natural restrictions which produce narrow trains of thought. Also to develop drawing and presentation skills.

Resources

Exercise books
HB pencils
Coloured pencils
A number of grids
Wooden blocks 50 mm × 25 mm × 25 mm
Fine-tipped, black felt-tip pens

Content

Issue grids and blocks to students who are allowed to work in small groups of two or three. Also issue sets of instructions and have a class discussion to ensure that all of the students understand them fully.

I have usually found it necessary to gather the students around me to discuss the instructions whilst demonstrating the various solutions to the first problem. First of all, build a low tower which is only 75 mm high and 50 mm by 50 mm all the way up to the top. Then with reference to the instructions such as 'Does it say that the tower has to be 50 mm wide and 50 mm long all the way up to the top?' 'Does it say in the instructions that the base of the tower must be a square?' I encourage students to give me suggestions as to how to increase the height of the tower.

Issue the second tower problem, without the solutions, and ask them to answer the problem using the grid and bricks. After a short period of time, find out which group has produced the tallest tower and share ideas around the class. Then inform the group of the height that I have achieved (see page 29). If my tower is taller, ask the students to try again.

When the highest solution, or solutions, have been produced, share the ideas, once again, around the group. Then ask the students to produce an isometric sketch of their final solution in their exercise books.

Issue the third tower problem etc.

Assignment

Apply colour and tone to the sketchwork.

Teacher Notes

We are normally taught by the use of patterns, which means we are familiar with a process and are able to repeat it when it is appropriate. This style of teaching, however, tends to make us reliant on these processes which have been given to us to memorise. It is difficult to produce our own patterns or processes because we have not had the experience or practice.

If we are faced with a problem, we immediately look for a pattern we recognise and if one appears which is acceptable, we are then satisfied and the process stops. If a solution is not obvious, and a suitable pattern does not occur to us, so we see no way to proceed, lateral thinking can often be a useful alternative way to continue with our efforts of finding a solution.

> 'Lateral thinking is made necessary by the limitations of vertical thinking. The terms 'lateral' and 'vertical' were suggested by the following considerations.
>
> It is not possible to dig a hole in a different place by digging the same hole deeper.
>
> Logic is the tool that is used to dig holes deeper and bigger, to make them altogether better holes. But if the hole is in the wrong place, then no amount of improvement is going to put it in the right place. No matter how obvious this may seem to every digger, it is still easier to go on digging in the same hole than to start all over again in a new place. Vertical thinking is digging the same hole deeper; lateral thinking is to try again elsewhere.'
>
> *Edward de Bono* (1967)

The ability to break away from conventional thinking techniques is very difficult because we spend most of our time memorising facts and figures without too much understanding. Another fault in our education system is the lack of attention given to doing things for ourselves. Experimentation can help us to understand things better and gives the opportunity for new patterns and techniques to be discovered.

Edward de Bono (1968 and 1969) devised the de Bono block problem. This exercise was used to develop sequential thinking, but I found that pupils gave in very quickly when they could not find a quick solution. Although several solutions were possible for each of the various parts of the exercise, there were no simple, intermediate stages. Each solution was either right or wrong. This prompted me to try to produce a different block problem, where various levels of success could be achieved, and each level could then be built upon. Thus all students, by achieving some success, would hopefully be encouraged enough to develop their ideas further and find better, or at least, alternative solutions. The 'Six Block Tower Problem' allows some success to be achieved by using familiar patterns, but if greater heights are to be reached there has to be some movement away from our natural constraints.

I advocate that one should never be fully satisfied with a solution to any problem and to question every process, including all of my suggestions in this book, to see if different or better ones can be found. These are essential stages in the development of the problem-solving process.

My approach to the Block Problem can be found on pages 24 and 27, and a list of heights achieved as well as the solutions on pages 29-35.

Hank Kahney says (1986) 'You might find it incredible that researchers think that they can learn anything about real-world problem-solving by creating "toy worlds" – puzzle-like tasks such as the Towers of Hanoi problem.' and 'This is like engineers making small models for use in wind tunnels. All sciences create "toy worlds" for close examination, mainly because the real world is very complex and messy. As psychologists we are interested in what we learn from studying toy worlds only to the extent that it helps us to understand how people behave in the real world, which is the actual focus of our interest.'

At the conclusion of the tower problems it is useful to have a class discussion to make the students aware of which constraints prevented them from immediately producing the tallest tower and any new strategies they may have acquired. The self-imposed restrictions are usually highlighted in these discussions; for example, they thought it had to be done in a certain way, or they had not fully understood the situation and they lacked creativity.

INSTONE'S 6-BLOCK TOWER PROBLEM

Materials Required:

1. Six blocks of wood measuring 50 mm × 25 mm × 25 mm.
2. One sheet of paper or card 150 mm × 150 mm divided into thirty-six 25 mm × 25 mm squares.

Instructions

The following information applies to each of the problems given below.

Do not be satisfied with your first attempt.

All of the six blocks must contact at least one other and must stand up without additional support, except from the other blocks.

The contact of two blocks can be minimal as long as they are touching.

All blocks must be placed in a horizontal or vertical plane.

There must be a minimum of 25 mm block contact with each of the four sides of the imaginary squares of 50 mm, 75 mm, 100 mm, 125 mm, 125+mm and 150 mm stated in the following problems. For example, in the diagram shown below, the block has been placed on the square so that it has a length and width measurement of 50 mm. That is, the two axes are at 90° to each other and could be defined as length and width measurements. However, this would NOT be acceptable in the following problems, because it does not meet the requirement of a minimum of 25 mm block contact on each of the four sides of the square.

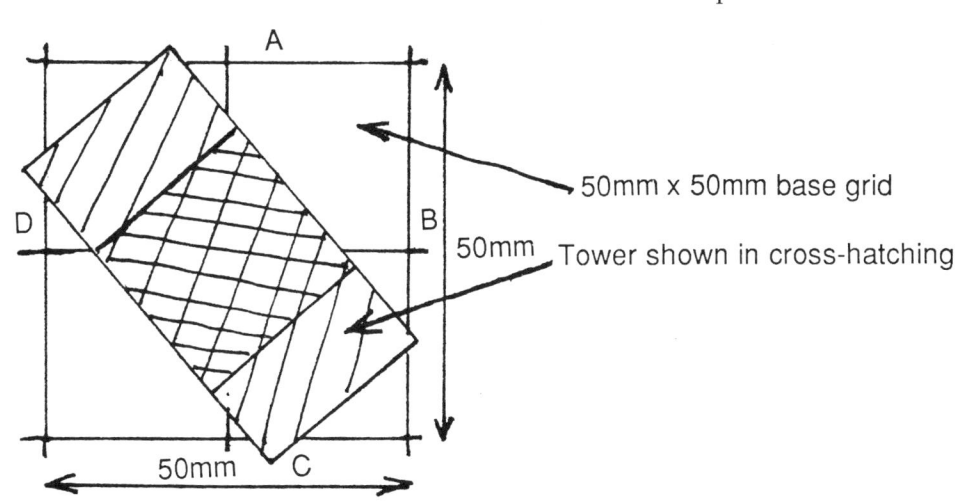

Once the length and width measurements have been achieved, the tower does not need to be these sizes all the way up.

(Although the plan of this tower has a minimum width and length measurement of 50 mm, it does not meet the requirement of having a minimum of 25 mm block contact on each of the four sides of the square ABCD.)

When you have produced your tallest tower, before looking at the pictorial solutions, only look at the heights which can be achieved. If you have not reached the height given, try again.

The heights which can be produced are shown on page 29.

Perhaps you can produce even taller towers than the solutions which are given.

Problem 1

Construct the tallest tower possible, containing a minimum width and length measurement of 50 mm and comply with the given instructions.

Problem 2

Construct the tallest tower possible, containing a minimum width and length measurement of 75 mm and comply with the given instructions.

Problem 3

Construct the tallest tower possible, containing a minimum width and length measurement of 100 mm and comply with the given instructions.

Problem 4

Construct the tallest tower possible, containing a minimum width and length measurement of 125 mm and comply with the given instructions.

Problem 5

Construct the tallest tower possible, containing a minimum width and length measurement of more than 125 mm and comply with the given instructions.

Then try a tower with a width and length measurement of 150 mm which complies with the given instructions.

The Grid

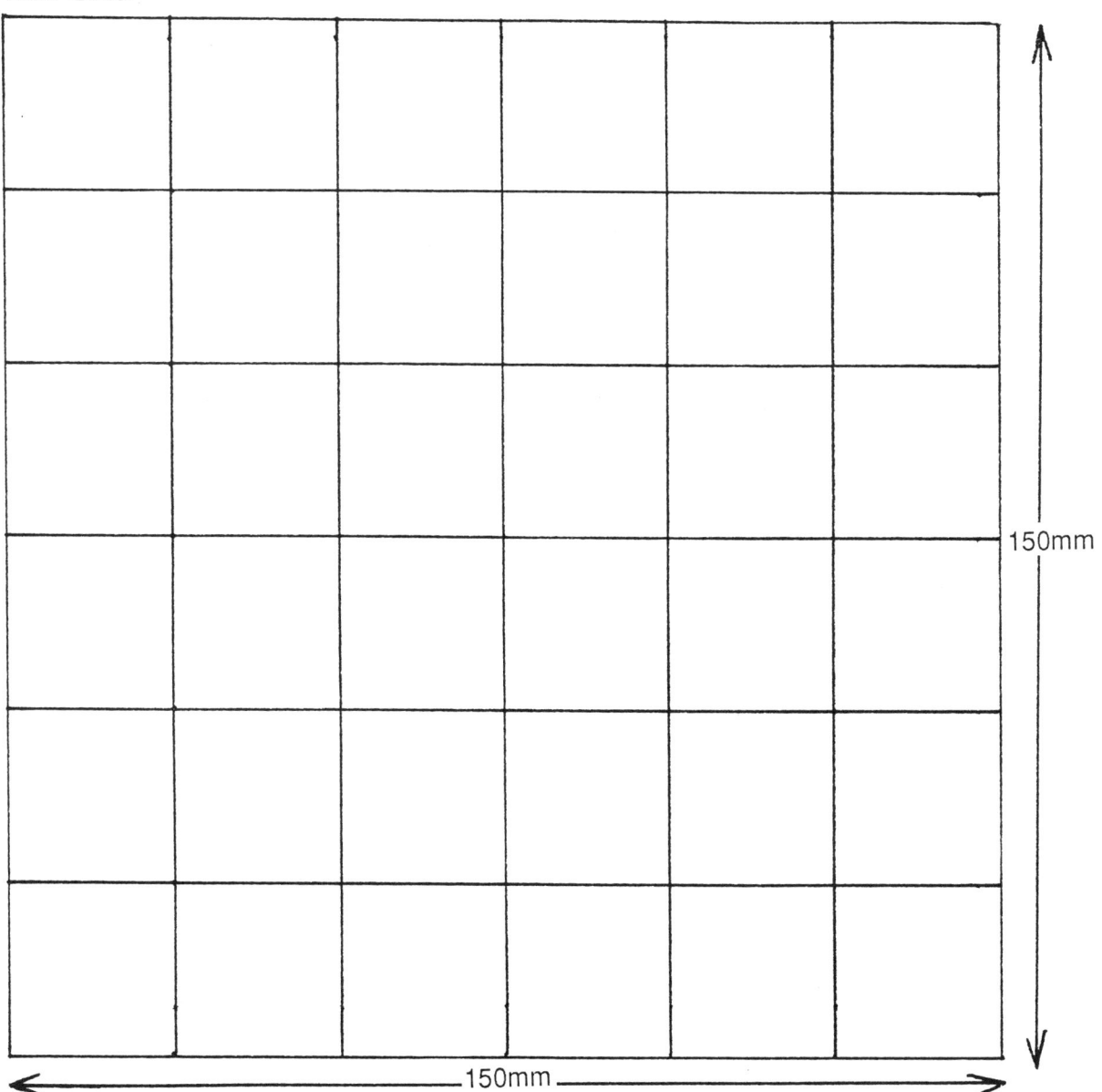

(150mm × 150mm grid)

Heights which can be achieved in Problems 1 to 5 of the tower problem

Problem 1
250 mm

Problem 2
225 mm

Problem 3
200 mm

Problem 4
175 mm

Problem 5
175 mm

The tallest tower shown in the pictorial solutions with a minimum width and length of 150 mm is 125 mm. (It *is* possible to go higher.)

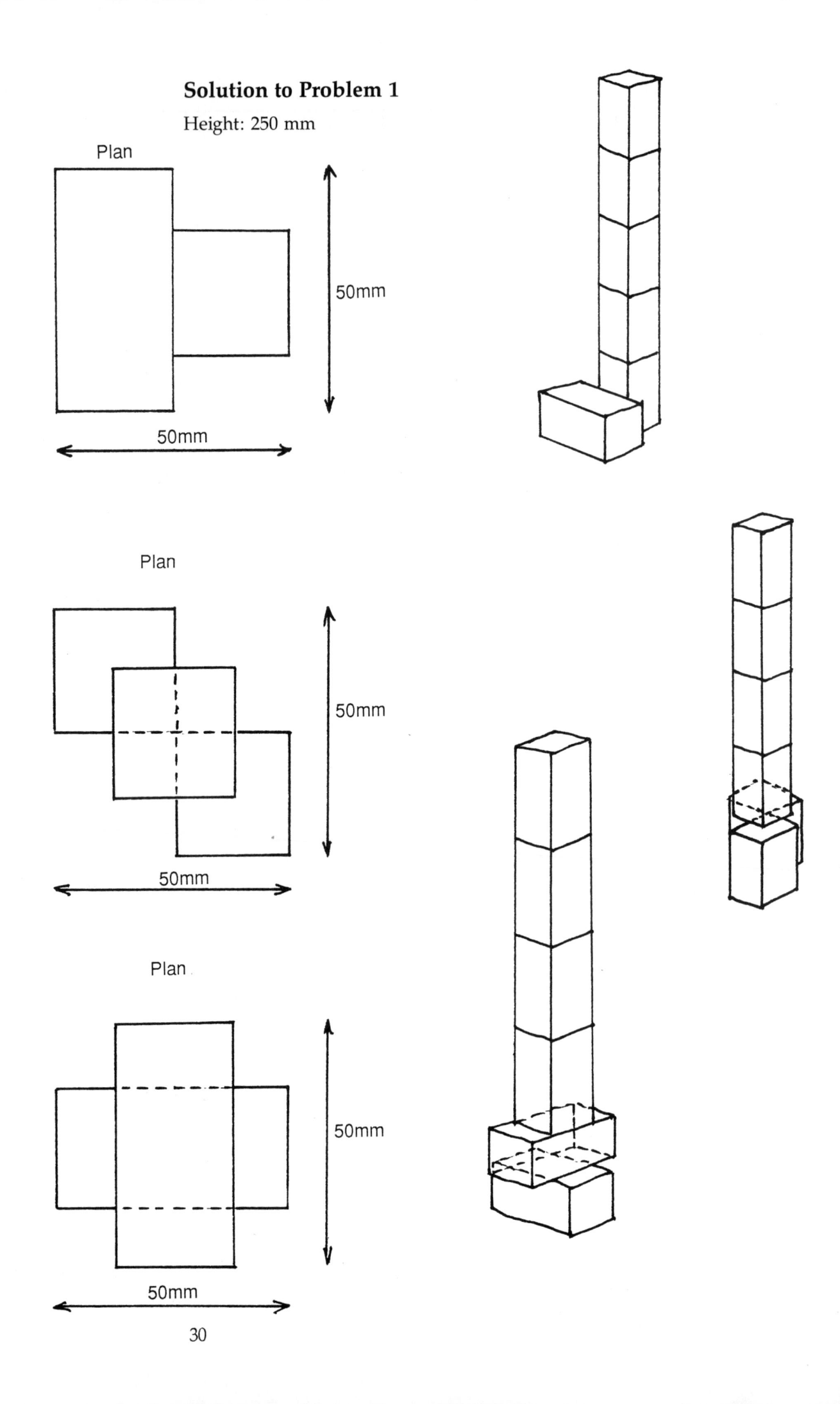

Solution to Problem 1

Height: 250 mm

Plan

50mm

50mm

Plan

50mm

50mm

Plan

50mm

50mm

Solution to Problem 2

Height: 225 mm

Plan

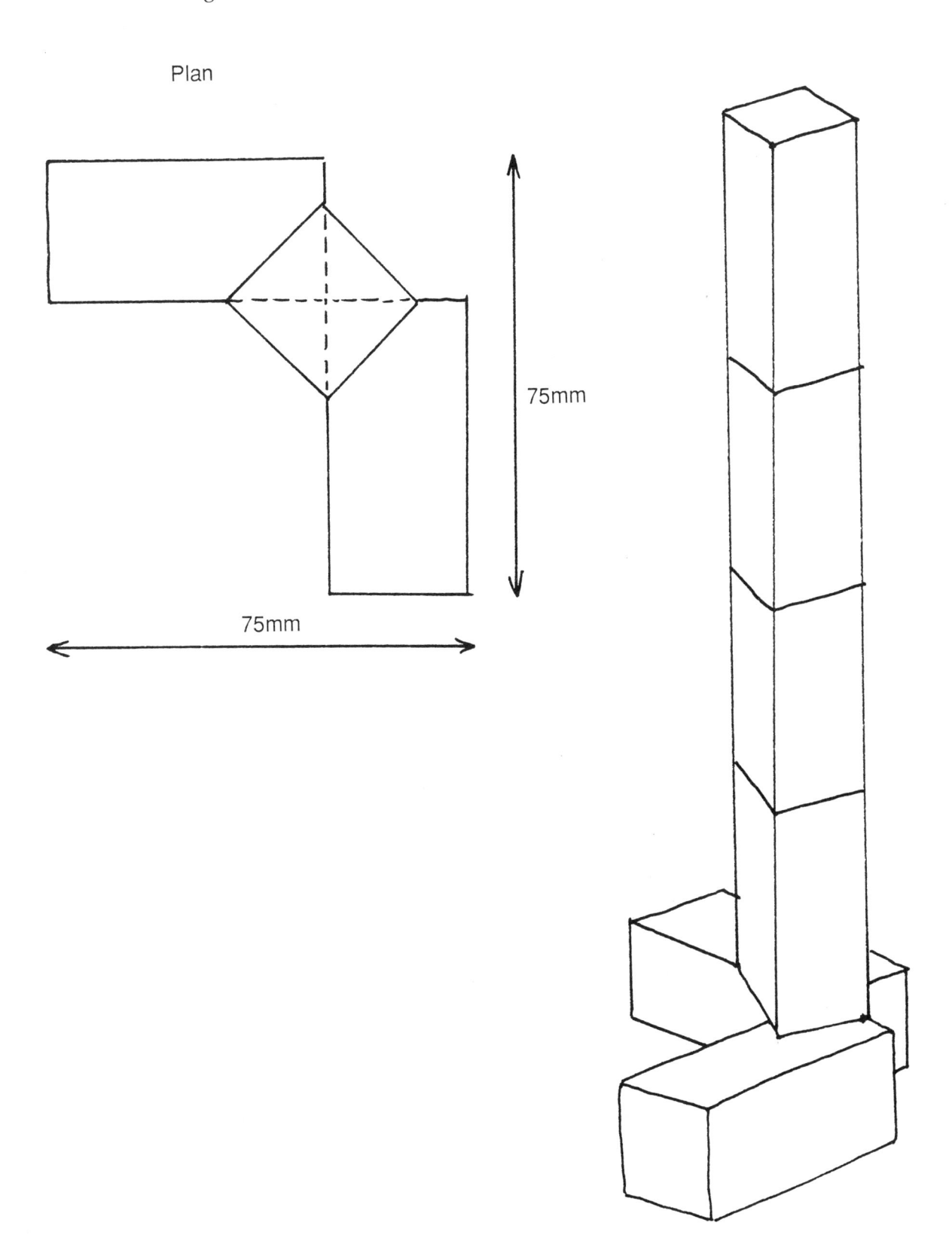

75mm

75mm

Solution to Problem 3

Height: 200 mm

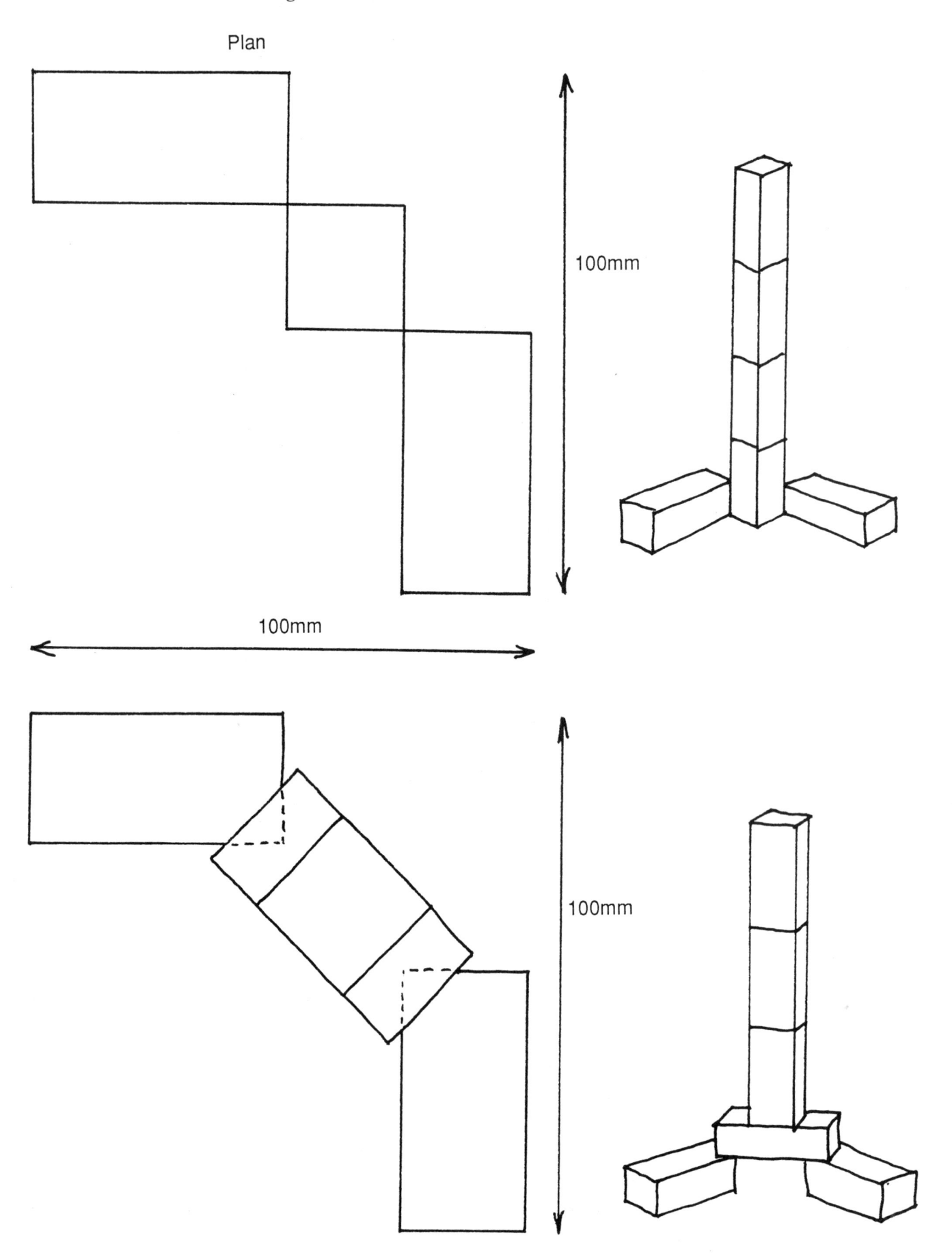

Plan

100mm

100mm

100mm

Solution to Problem 4

Height: 175 mm

The first diagram shown below is a good solution but only reaches a height of 150 mm. However if the central block is angled, as shown in the second diagram below, the height can be increased to 175 mm.

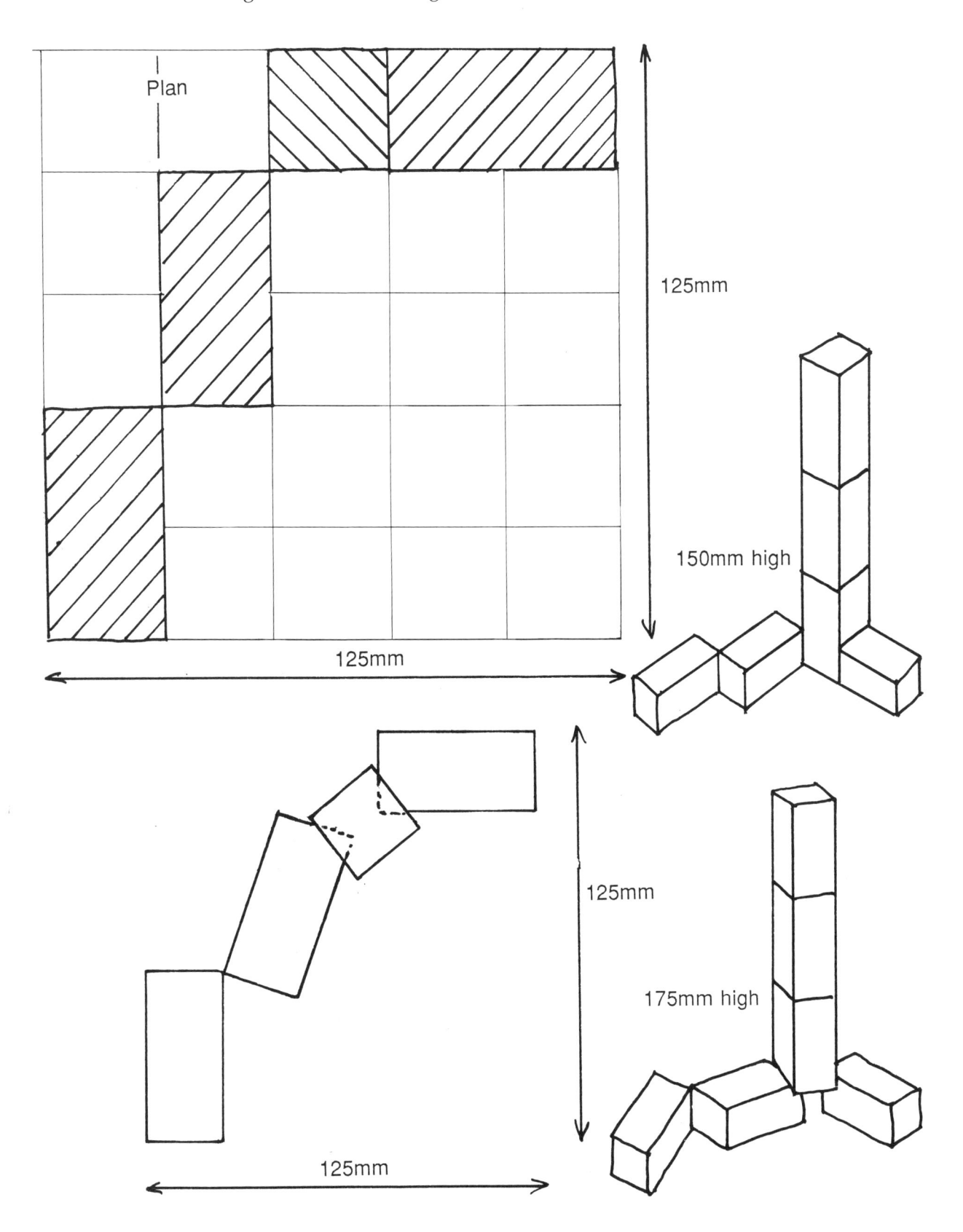

Solution to Problem 5

Height: 175 mm

It is important to note that the width and length need to be over 125 mm but not necessarily 150 mm.

The first diagram shown below is a good solution but only reaches a height of 150 mm. However, it can be seen that the top block is well over the 125 mm dimension and could be brought in nearer to the 125 mm square and still produce a tower over the minimum dimension. This would enable the central tower to be elevated another 25 mm by supporting it on top of two other bricks, as shown in the second diagram.

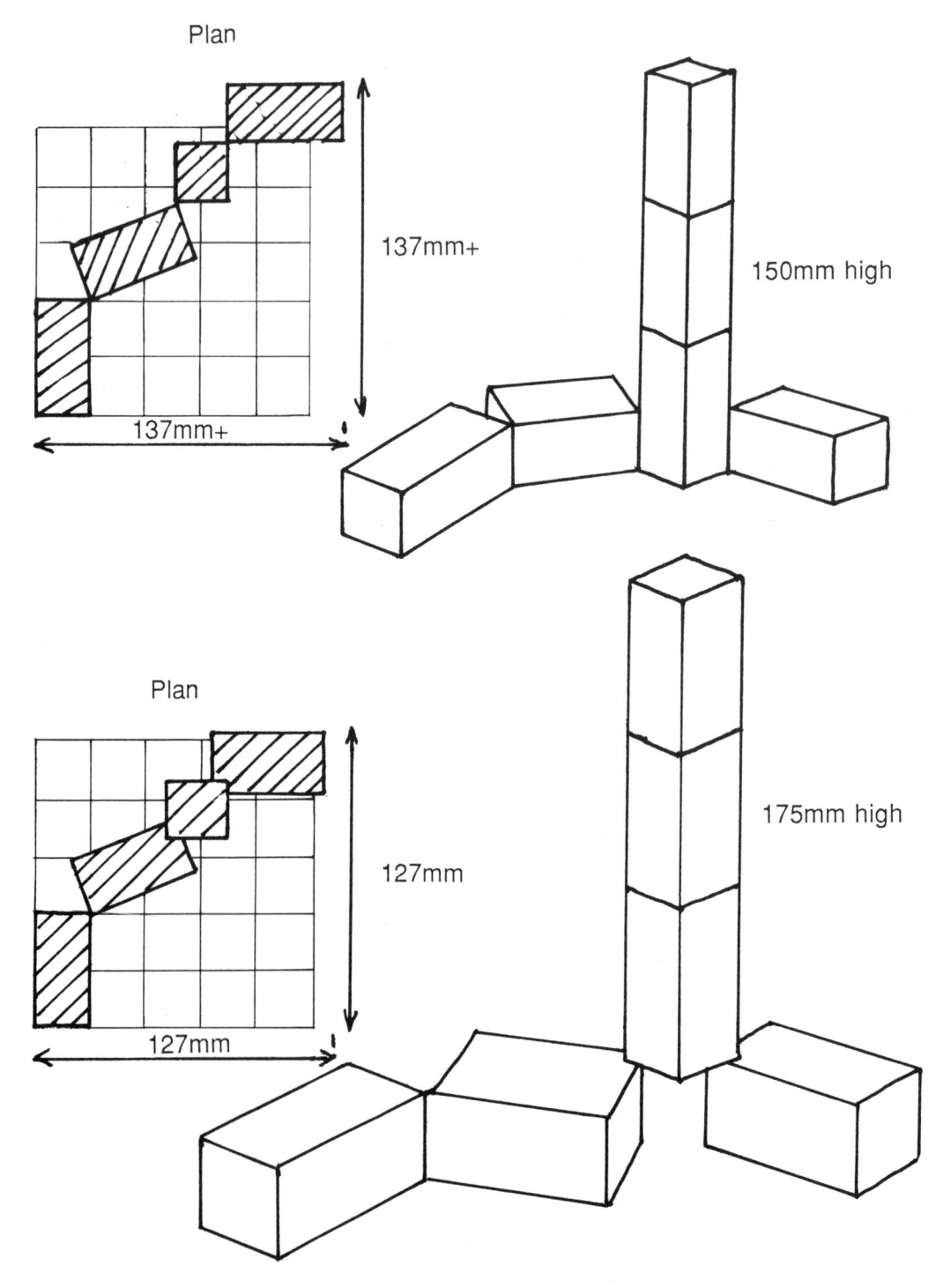

The diagram shown below gives one solution for a tower which can be produced from a minimum width and length of 150 mm. This produces a height of only 125 mm. (It *is* possible to produce a higher one.)

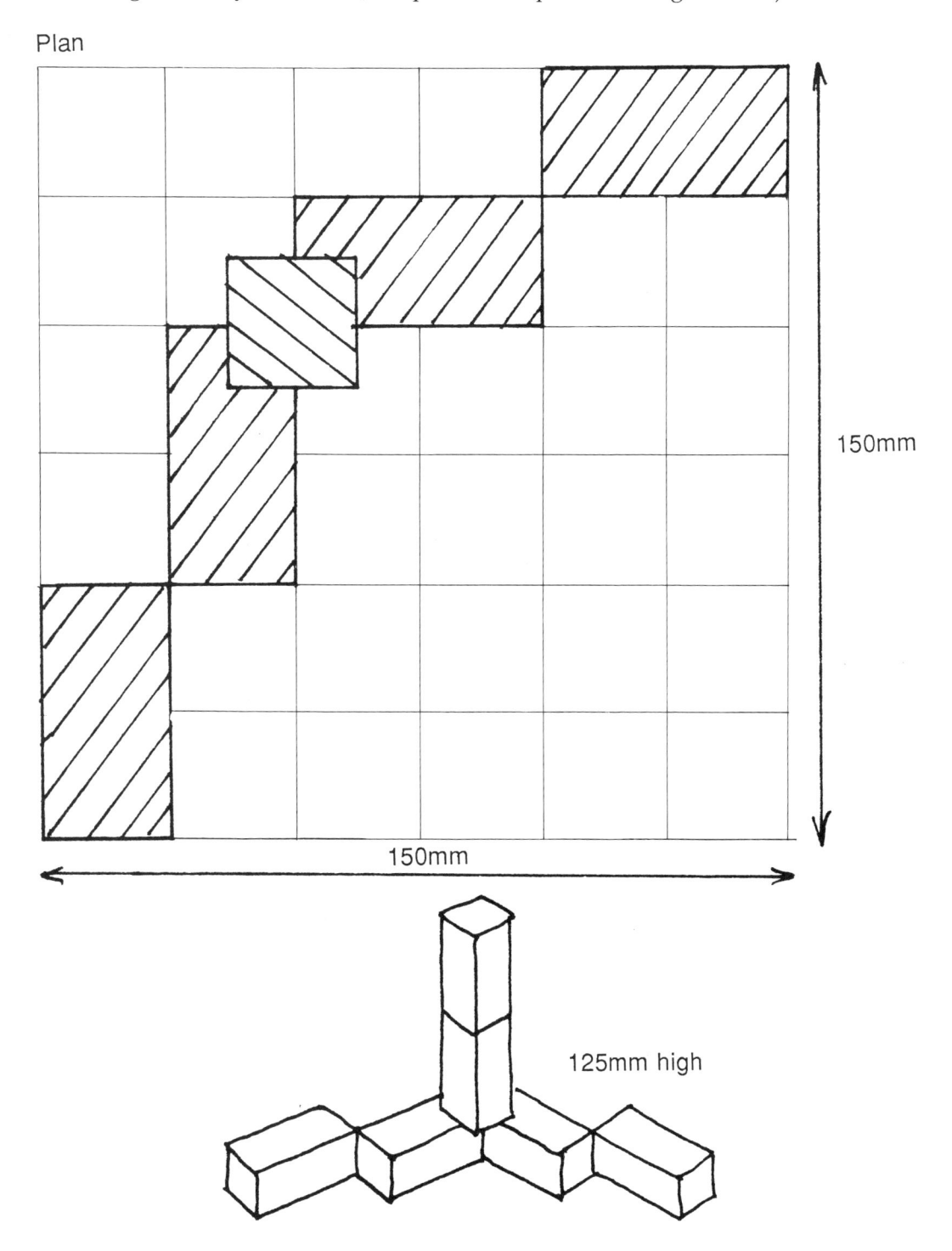

Plan

150mm

150mm

125mm high

LESSON 6: CREATIVE, DIVERGENT AND LATERAL THINKING

Objective

To help students break away from traditional patterns of thought by developing the use of the imagination and encouraging creativity.

Resources

Exercise books
Newspaper
Clothes peg (dolly type)
Margarine tub
Pencil
Plastic bag
Matchbox
Length of sellotape
Paper clip
Washing up liquid bottle
Wooden cotton reel

Content

Divide the class into small groups of two or three and issue each group with one of the above items. Alternatively, some items of your own choice may be selected.

Working as individuals, the students are asked to write down as many alternative uses as possible for each item in the short time allocated for examination.

Move items around every four or five minutes.

It should be pointed out at this stage that we have a natural reluctance to reject ideas because they appear, at first glance, to be silly. This tendency we have, as 'convergent thinkers', is mentioned in the Problem-Solving Module of the Schools Council Modular Courses in Technology (1982):

> 'Thus, whereas "convergent thinkers" may have thought of using a brick as a book-end, a piece of sculpture, a hammer, a pendulum, a footwiper and so on, they have rejected these ideas as foolish ones and not written them down, until told otherwise. This shows that many of us are reluctant to put forward what at first sight may seem to be a foolish solution. Sometimes a simple solution to a problem has been held up for this reason . . .
>
> Do not reject ideas until they have been fully evaluated.'

The influence of the normal use of the item will also have a detrimental effect on the students' abilities to think creatively. I have found that this can be overcome to some extent by following some of the techniques which follow.

Assignment

Cut the cake, shown below, into eight pieces using three cuts only.

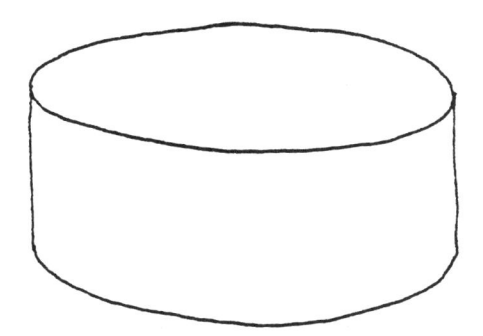

Teacher Notes

It is important to note that it is human nature to take things for granted and to start questioning things only when it is too late, if they are questioned at all. Questioning everything is an essential part of developing the ability to think.

Many of the students will take it for granted that the chosen items may not be broken in half, cut up, drilled, only part of them used, or several of them used together, etc. If they are not made aware of all these possibilities and more, it will restrict the number of ideas they produce.

I also find it very useful to choose various activities such as gardening, fishing, cookery, wall papering or playing and then ask myself, could the object or part of it be used in some of these areas? Perhaps you can produce other ways of helping the students to be more creative with this task.

I have found that the less able students, who are quite often the jokers in the group, often tend to produce the best and by far the largest list of alternative uses for the objects. This could be because they had been affected less by traditional teaching, which gave them more freedom in their ability to be creative. It could also be that through their skill at making funny remarks about everything, which is a developed use of lateral thinking, they were able to transfer this skill to being creative in other areas. It could be a combination of both.

It is very difficult to make yourself question things that we have always taken for granted, but in order to develop creative thinking skills this needs to be done.

Let us examine a simple addition problem. Can we devise another way of adding? It does not matter if we are unable to produce a *better* method but finding alternative solutions can be very satisfying at the same time as developing creativity and a deeper understanding of the situation. We tend to take for granted that the methods we were taught at school were the best and perhaps the only ways of dealing with situations and consequently do not bother to question them. Traditional education does not require us to question or experiment with method and, furthermore, does not allow time for such practices to occur in its rigid examination time schedule. However, what about the addition problem? The traditional way to add 6 and 7 would be:

```
  6
+ 7
―――
 13
```

Let us now tackle this same problem by using subtraction as part of the process and only adding together units of one. This method requires each number to be taken away from a ten and these two additional single ten units added together to produce two ten units, or twenty. Then more subtraction occurs because you then take away from twenty the two new numbers obtained from the first subtraction. This produces the same answer of thirteen. For example:

Stage 1	Stage 2	Stage 3	Stage 4
6	$10 - 6 = 4$	$20 - 4 = 16$	$16 - 3 = 13$
+7	$10 - 7 = 3$		
――	20		

Here is another example of this technique using a larger pair of numbers. This time the numbers have to be taken from one hundred units.

Stage 1	Stage 2	Stage 3	Stage 4
26	$100 - 26 = 74$	$200 - 74 = 126$	$126 - 85 = 41$
+15	$100 - 15 = 85$		
――	200		

Perhaps you can find some other way of adding.

Although the above method works it is a more time-consuming process and in its present form does not challenge the normal method. However, with more examination and experimentation one might be able to produce an alternative to the traditional method of addition.

Challenging accepted ways of doing anything develops creativity and gives one a better understanding of the various processes and why they remain the same, or why they should change.

Another example of the constraints caused by people taking things for granted can be shown in the cake problem. If we examine two of the major elements in this situation, the cake and the cut, we find that most people assume that firstly the cake, or pieces of cake after the first cut, cannot be moved about. They assume secondly that the cut has to be produced by a knife which must be a straight one and thirdly, that all the pieces of cake must be the same size or shape. The students who develop an awareness to the constraints will be the ones who will manage to be the most creative because their skills at lateral thinking will develop, increasing their abilities to find alternative solutions.

Some possible solutions are shown below. They follow the examples of alternative uses for everyday objects.

Alternative Uses for Everyday Objects

Check the answers at the end and give a mark for each 'original' answer. Only give one mark for similar answers, for example, the margarine tub could be used to store nails, hold maggots, store sugar etc. All these are similar and only warrant a total of one mark.

Examples of Objects and Answers

Note that some of the best solutions were produced when lateral and divergent thinking techniques were applied.

(a) Newspaper: insulation, blotting paper, packing

(b) Clothes peg (dolly type): fork, hair curler, three laid radially for a pan stand, writing (convert to charcoal), plant labels (when broken in half), fishing float, record rack, beads and marbles (tops removed)

(c) Margarine tub: jelly mould, storage container, slice into circles for a hoop game, string telephone, timing device (water and small hole), plant pot stand, whizzer (lid)

(d) Pencil: bedding for a hamster (use a pencil sharpener to convert it to shavings), fishing float, dibber, throwing dart (attach flights), electric contact points

(e) Plastic bag: rain coat, rain hat, icing piping bag, sledge, bivvy bag, tent, kite, small greenhouse, bandage, funnel, windscreen

(f) Matchbox: nail file, storage units, napkin ring, protective mat (several glued together), stamp for producing rectangles

(g) Elastic band: finger bandage, weighing device, ball, musical instrument

(h) Length of sellotape: plaster to stop bleeding, keeping items clean, strengthening items, labelling

(i) Paper clip: fishing hook, several to make a chain, spring, plant tie

(j) Washing up liquid bottle: pastry cutter, scoop, hydraulic pump, funnel, rolling pin, candle holder, bird feeder

(k) Wooden cotton reel: pike float, stamp, pencil holder, beads, pulley, spinning top

Possible Solutions to the Cake Problem

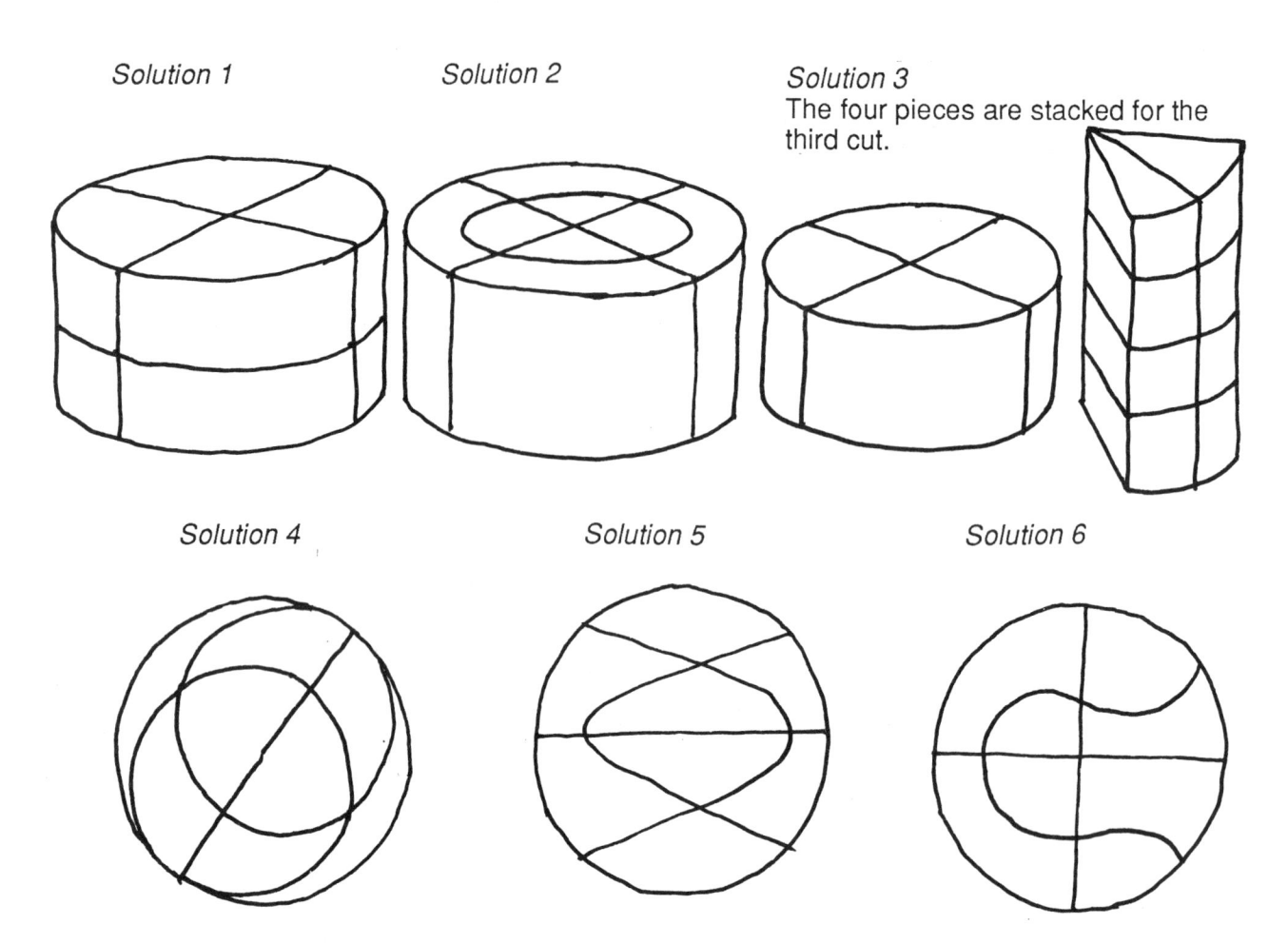

Solution 1

Solution 2

Solution 3
The four pieces are stacked for the third cut.

Solution 4

Solution 5

Solution 6

The following solution divides the cake into ten pieces only using three cuts.

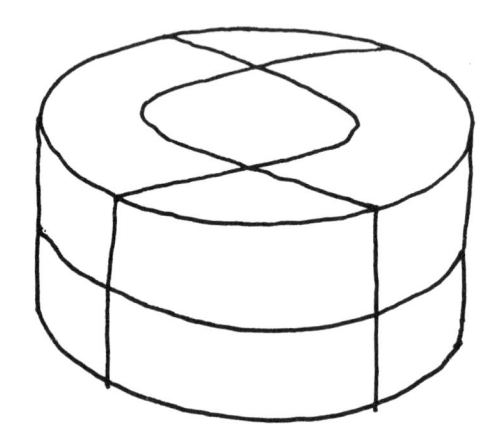

LESSON 7: CREATIVE AND LATERAL THINKING I

Objective

To develop the use of the imagination and give the pupils more practice with lateral thinking techniques.

Also to practise communicative skills in the form of annotated sketchwork.

Resources

Initiative Tests
Coloured pencils
Exercise books

Content

Discuss the need to consider alternative solutions to problems and not to be satisfied with the first idea that comes into the head.

Develop positive and creative thinking techniques.

Issue Initiative Test 3 (page 52) to each student.

Solutions should be sketched, coloured (if appropriate), and a clear explanation given at each of the stages.

Assignment

Issue Initiative Text 4 (page 54).

Teacher Notes

It is important to point out to the students that they should always assume that there could be more than one solution to any problem facing them, and that the first answer they produce may not always be the best one. Once we have found a solution to a situation, we tend to be satisfied and automatically switch off, or lose interest. Another fault to which many of us are prone, is the tendency to reject ideas too soon, before they have been fully explored, especially if they appear at first glance to be unacceptable.

To illustrate this tendency show the students the picture on page 43 of the upside-down frying pan which is placed on a gas cooker. Ask the students to comment about the situation. Invariably all of the comments turn out to be critical or negative, thus highlighting my earlier point of automatic rejection when something fits into the category of being incorrect.

We need to apply positive or constructive thinking to all situations, even though they may appear impossible or unacceptable at first.

Once this tendency to be critical has been pointed out to the students, they can then be asked to look for unusual or beneficial consequences which the pan situation can stimulate.

Some positive comments which have been made are:

1. The side of the pan which is being used for cooking could be easier to clean, because there are no difficult corners to reach.
2. Perhaps the rim of the pan would retain more heat and result in more energy being saved.
3. You would not be able to use more than a thin smear of fat for frying or it would run off the edge of the pan. This could result in people using less fat in their cooking.

If we consider the above ideas in designing a different frying pan, we could produce a shallow dish with a rim around the bottom and an overflow system for excess fat.

This technique of looking for positive or beneficial aspects of a situation which would normally be rejected, can develop a much broader base for the development of thinking skills.

In Initiative Test 3, there are several ways of achieving the final goal, which is to reach the way out. The tendency, as mentioned above, will be for the students to produce and be satisfied with the first idea that comes into their head. Once again point this out and ask them to consider various approaches to each of the obstacles before deciding on their best choice of action. The first solution may work but it is not always the best.

Another fault many of us have is that we are satisfied with any result, as long as it works. Consequently, we do not want to look any further for alternative courses of action.

Typical questions one could ask about the situations to be faced in Initiative Test 3, which may stimulate ideas, are:

1. Are you being influenced by the obvious?
2. Are you considering all the available elements?
3. Are you trying to reach the easiest crossing point?
4. Do you need to use as many of the available items as you may possibly be considering?

The Inverted Frying Pan

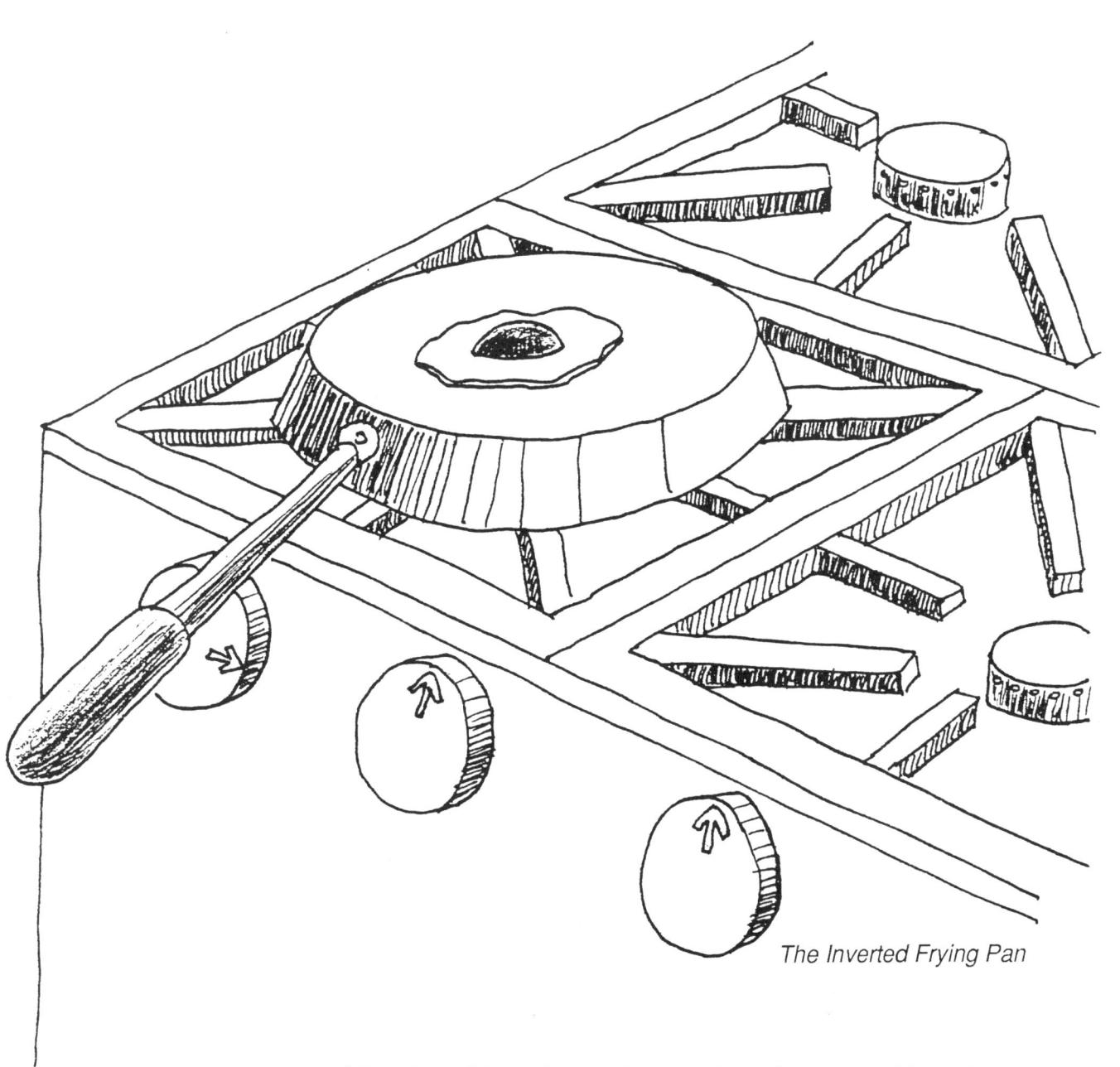

'Negative criticism is easy because it is always possible to find fault with anything if one looks hard enough. It is quite easy to concentrate on the faults and ignore what is worthwhile. But the main and overriding attraction of criticism is that it at once makes the critic superior to what he is criticising . . .

Because criticism is so easy it is often the refuge of mediocre minds who cannot be interesting in any other way. Too often a critic forgets that he is not criticising the situation but only his understanding of it . . .

In practice you do not have to understand something to criticise it — indeed, criticism is very often a camouflage for lack of understanding.'

Edward de Bono (1977)

LESSON 8: DEVELOPMENT OF INTUITIVE AND EMPIRICAL THINKING SKILLS

Objective

To use a practical situation to develop intuitive and empirical thinking, as well as the analytical process.

In addition, further practice in communication skills in the form of annotated sketchwork.

Resources

A4 plain paper and cartridge paper
A4 thin card – manila
Scissors
Pencils
Craft knives
Cutting boards
Rulers
6 rectangles of hardboard 125 mm × 75 mm × 4 mm, to act as mirrors

Content

Ask the students to make a device out of the piece of A4 card to hold steady a 125 mm × 75 mm mirror, whilst a man shaves. The device should be adjustable in the direction it can angle the mirror, and the whole item should not need any other materials, such as glue or sellotape, to hold it together.

Assignment

Issue the following problem: A headmaster in a junior school decides to find out who is the best chess player in that school. There is a total of 10 classes, 5 of which have 25 pupils in each and the remaining 5, 27 per group. Each class organises a knockout competition to find the best player, then the winner from each of the 10 groups goes forward into the final knockout competition. What is the total number of matches played in the school before the winner is found?

Teacher Notes

I have found it important at this stage to introduce some practical work to help maintain some students' interest, especially the less able candidates.

It is also important to help students to tackle problems analytically and to adopt logical procedures in solving them. However, students must be allowed to make mistakes and spend some time working on 'red herrings' and following false scents during their exploratory work. To allow the skill in this area to develop in the student, it is important to resist the temptation to over-direct them. Never give what you consider to be the 'correct answer'.

It can be useful, before starting on this exercise, to spend a couple of periods in a practical situation, experimenting with card to try to discover as many ways as possible to fasten it together without the aid of glue, sellotape, pins, etc. A knowledge of the construction of a cone from a flat piece of material could also be useful.

Several ways of joining card together are shown below; perhaps you can find even more methods.

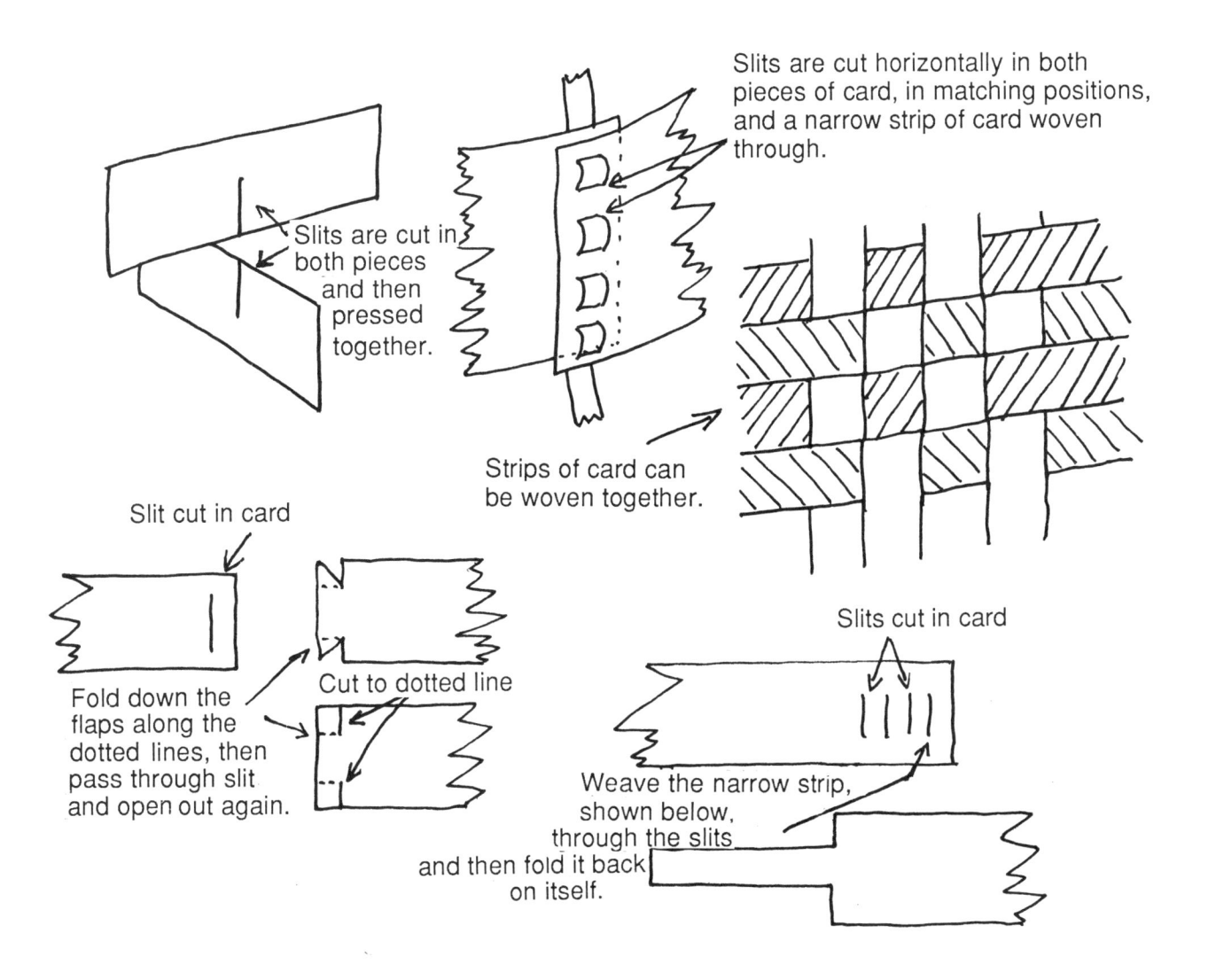

Slits are cut in both pieces and then pressed together.

Slits are cut horizontally in both pieces of card, in matching positions, and a narrow strip of card woven through.

Strips of card can be woven together.

Slit cut in card

Fold down the flaps along the dotted lines, then pass through slit and open out again.

Cut to dotted line

Slits cut in card

Weave the narrow strip, shown below, through the slits and then fold it back on itself.

The Mirror Support

After the students have been issued with the brief, they are then given a couple of sheets of plain, A4 paper, preferably cartridge quality.

Additional plain paper should also be made available for the students to produce rough sketches of ideas they may wish to try out at a later stage.

It is important that each student produces several different ideas and makes acceptable, annotated pictorial sketches in an exercise book. These should be shaded and show details of construction and be followed by a brief evaluation.

Before the practical exercise starts it is important to make an analysis of the situation. This helps to stimulate directions to follow and techniques with which to experiment. This work should be tackled in exercise books. An example of some analysis and research is shown below:

Analysis and Research

1. How could the mirror be supported by this item?
   (a) Free standing
   (b) Hanging support

2. Does it need to be the same size or shape as the mirror?

3. How can the strength of card be increased?
   (a) Folding, bending, rolling
   (b) Laminating
   (c) Using it on its edge when folded, bent or rolled
   (d) Corrugating

4. Which processes can be done with card?
   (a) Cut
   (b) Pierced
   (c) Woven
   (d) Folded, bent, rolled
   (e) Pulped
   (f) Embossed
   (g) Scored

When the students have produced several different ideas through evaluation and practical experimentation, they should be able to choose their best solutions and make them out of manila card.

After the models have been made, the whole class should group together and watch each of the models being tested. A brief class discussion should take place about each of the solutions, to share ideas about how each model meets the requirements and how improvements could be made.

The students should then take their mirror supports away and in their exercise books write a brief final evaluation about their solution.

Solution to Knockout Chess Problem

There is a very quick solution to this problem if you do not follow the normal thought pattern, which is to concentrate your efforts on trying to produce a winner. If your attention is guided to considering the majority of the competitors, the losers, a solution begins to develop. This is because a loser is produced every time a game is played, and since there are 260 pupils in the school, all playing in the competition, 259 of them will lose. Because a loser is produced every match, and there are 259 losers, there must automatically be 259 games played to produce the final winner.

LESSON 9: CREATIVE AND LATERAL THINKING II

Objective

To give further practice in developing the use of the imagination and lateral thinking techniques.

To extend the development of communicative skills in the form of annotated sketchwork.

Resources

Initiative tests
Coloured pencils
Exercise books

Content

Issue Initiative Test 5 (page 56) to each student.

Solutions should be sketched and shaded (if appropriate), and a clear explanation given.

Ask the students to produce as many solutions as they can find, recording them all.

Issue Initiative Test 6 (page 58) to each student.

Assignment

Ask the students to produce as many different possible solutions to the problem of opening a tin of paint if no form of lever is available, such as a screwdriver, spoon, scissors, knife, etc.

Teacher Notes

There are some logical thinkers who do not accept that there is such a process as lateral thinking. They believe that all problems are solved by applying logic, even when they are faced with the type of problem which appears to have no obvious direction, and are delayed, or even prevented, from finding a solution.

The creative, lateral thinker, who has the ability to escape from following familiar thought patterns, can quite often find a solution more quickly from what appears at first glance to be impossible. However, if you present a different solution to a logical thinker, he or she would probably respond by showing a logical way of arriving at the same solution, even though he or she did not discover this idea for him/herself.

Having practised both styles of thinking, I have found that a temporary escape from logic is very useful, in that it develops more creativity, and does help one to find solutions to these difficult problems which appear logically impossible. I believe that if familiar patterns cannot be found immediately and commonsense applied, the natural tendency we have to take things for granted can seriously hamper any progress. A little lateral, creative thinking, combined with trial and error, can be a very useful tool in solving problems.

The second section of this book, which immediately follows this lesson, develops a logical process, which at the same time enables students to be more creative in problem-solving because it will give them a greater understanding of how to deal with problems in general.

The use of initiative tests not only gives the students practice in developing their thinking skills, but also develops their ability to communicate their ideas, both in graphic and written form. This ability to collate and convey information in a clear way is essential if success is to be gained in the area of design work across the curriculum, and also as a very important life skill in conveying clearly information of any kind to other people.

Solutions to the Tin of Paint Problem

The basic assumption is that some sort of lever is needed. For example, knife, scissors, spoon.

Suppose none of these is available, or any other kind of lever, which would probably be the only type of solution that would be considered when using the normal pattern of thinking. The students must challenge the original assumption or facts; could the job be done without paint, or is a lever really necessary?

As mentioned earlier, creative thinking or lateral jumps can be very useful when one comes to a dead end.

Some other possibilities could be:
corkscrew,
tin,
suction,
strike or crush tin,
puncture tin and pour into another container,
gentle heat to blow off lid.

INITIATIVE TEST 1

The picture shows a corner house, whose boundary wall is only 300 mm high and easily stepped over. Consequently passers-by tend to take a short cut over the garden.

There is a limited amount of money available, but even if additional bricks were bought, there would only be enough to build the wall to a height of 450 mm: a height which is still easy to step over.

Write about, and sketch, as many different solutions to this situation as you can.

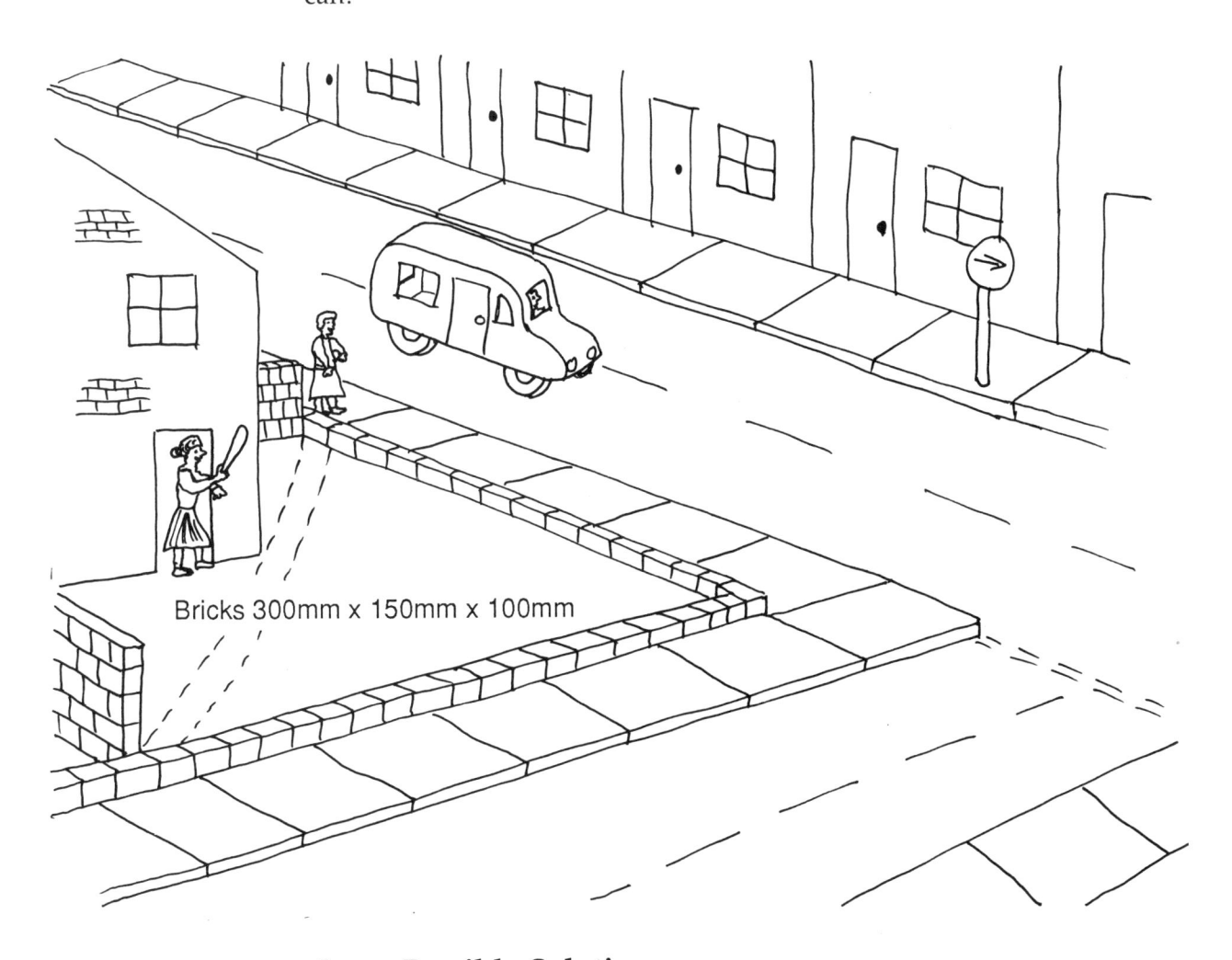

Bricks 300mm x 150mm x 100mm

Some Possible Solutions

Perhaps you can increase and improve this list.

1. Build up one side only. This would produce a wall 1200 mm high.
2. Build the wall higher all the way and leave spaces in between the bricks.
3. Buy some cheaper fencing material.
4. Move to another house.
5. Dig a wide trench along one side, to produce a ha-ha.
6. Prosecute people walking across.

7. Complain to the council.
8. Put a pond along one side.
9. Make it unpleasant for people to walk across. For example, keep it well dug, well watered to make it muddy, plant brambles or roses all over it, etc.
10. Plant a rose or blackthorn hedge.
11. Sell the garden to the council and have it made into a footpath.
12. Buy a dog.
13. Put a garage along one side.

INITIATIVE TEST 2

You have bought seven rolls of wallpaper to decorate your bedroom (diagram shown below). After measuring the walls, you discover that you need eight rolls. Unfortunately the shop has no more rolls of the same pattern paper and no one else stocks the same pattern. The paper was also old stock and can no longer be ordered and the shop closes down the following day. They will not exchange the paper or refund your money because they were reduced sale items. Another problem is that you only have enough money left to buy a maximum of four more rolls of wallpaper.

Write down or draw as many different solutions to the situation as you can.

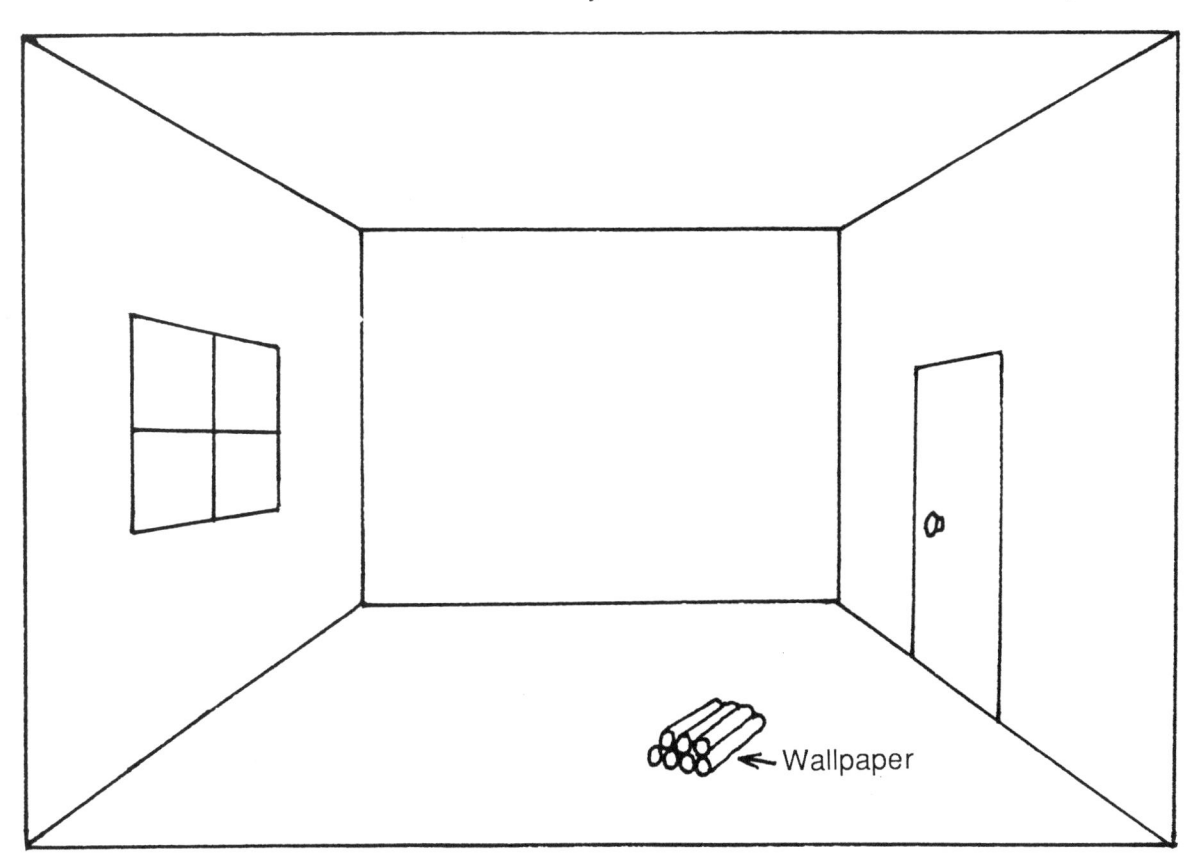

Some Possible Solutions

1. Decorate one wall with a different paper.

2. Put a panel of a different colour onto each wall.

3. Use a different colour paper on one wall, then emulsion all of the walls the same colour.

4. Do not decorate behind cupboards etc.

5. Do not decorate the wall up to the full height of the ceiling.

INITIATIVE TEST 3

The picture shows a man in a passage with the only direction of escape shown by the arrows on the wall, marked 'way out'.

A small platform is shown 3.1 m away from the starting point.

All the walls are perfectly flat and there is a vertical, smooth-sided drop to an unmeasured depth.

The only materials available to the man are the two boards and the two lengths of rope (sizes marked on picture).

With written work and diagrams, show how the man could successfully escape and not expose himself to any unnecessary danger.

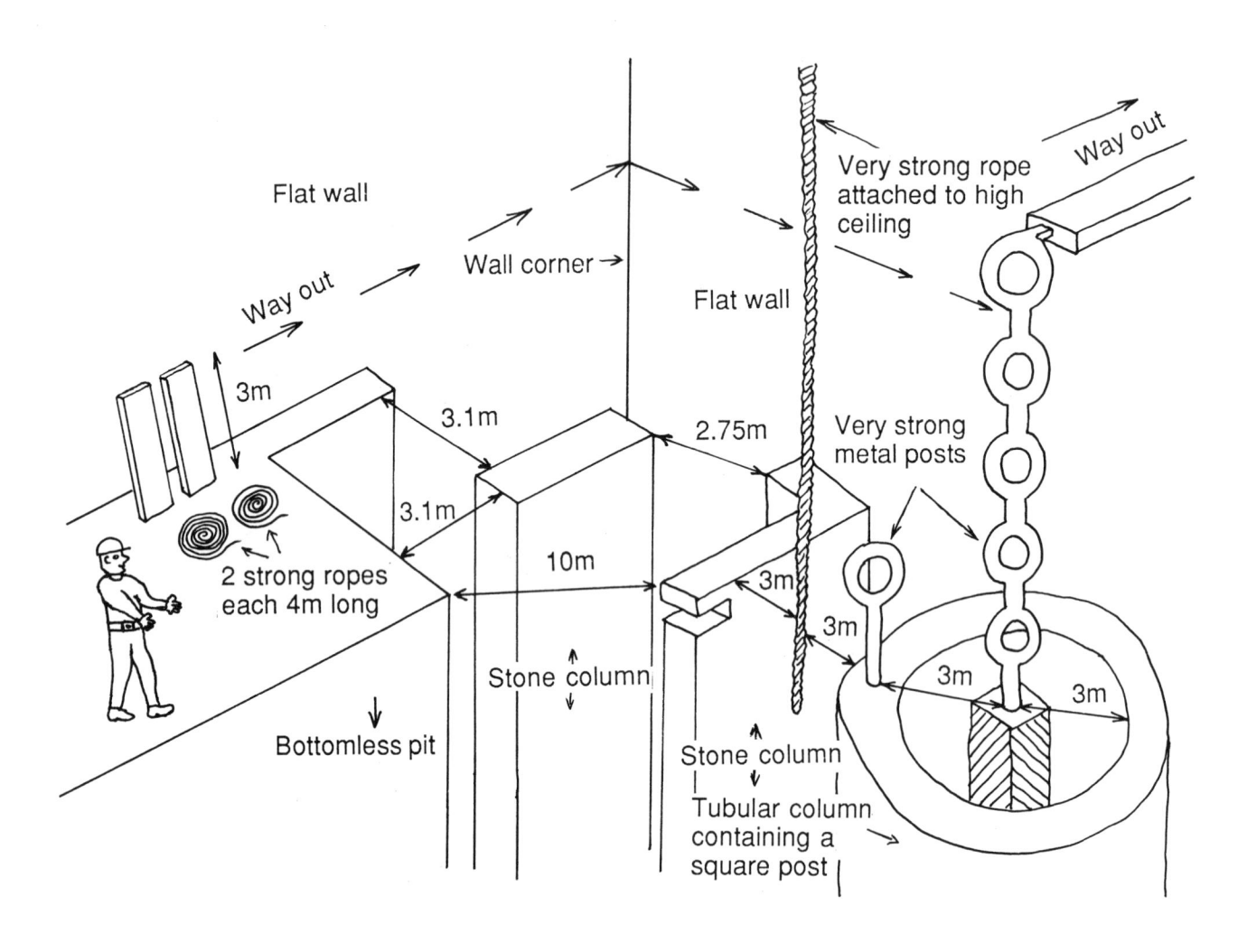

Some Possible Solutions

Perhaps you can find some better ones.

The two planks could be overlapped and tied together, then they would reach across. Or possibly a better solution is to lay planks A and B as shown in the diagram.

It is important to remember to take the ropes with you.

Plank A can be retrieved by attaching one end of one of the ropes to it before retrieving plank B.

The second obstacle can be easily overcome by laying plank A or B across the two columns.

By placing plank A or B into the gap in the column, you are enabled to walk out and reach the rope hanging from the ceiling. You can now swing across onto the circular column, remembering once again to take both of the ropes with you. If both of the two ropes are tied together and one end is firmly attached to the plank, it can be pulled across onto the circular column after you have swung across.

There are several ways of reaching the way out. If you did remember to retrieve the plank, it can simply be placed across the gap.

Or you could tie together the two ropes, tie one end onto the small post, then holding onto the other end, walk around the column. This of course will attach the rope around the central pillar. The second end of rope is now attached to the small post thus enabling you climb across, up and out.

A final method is to throw the rope over the plank at the top of the metal pillar, then tie a slip knot and pull it tight. You can then climb up and out.

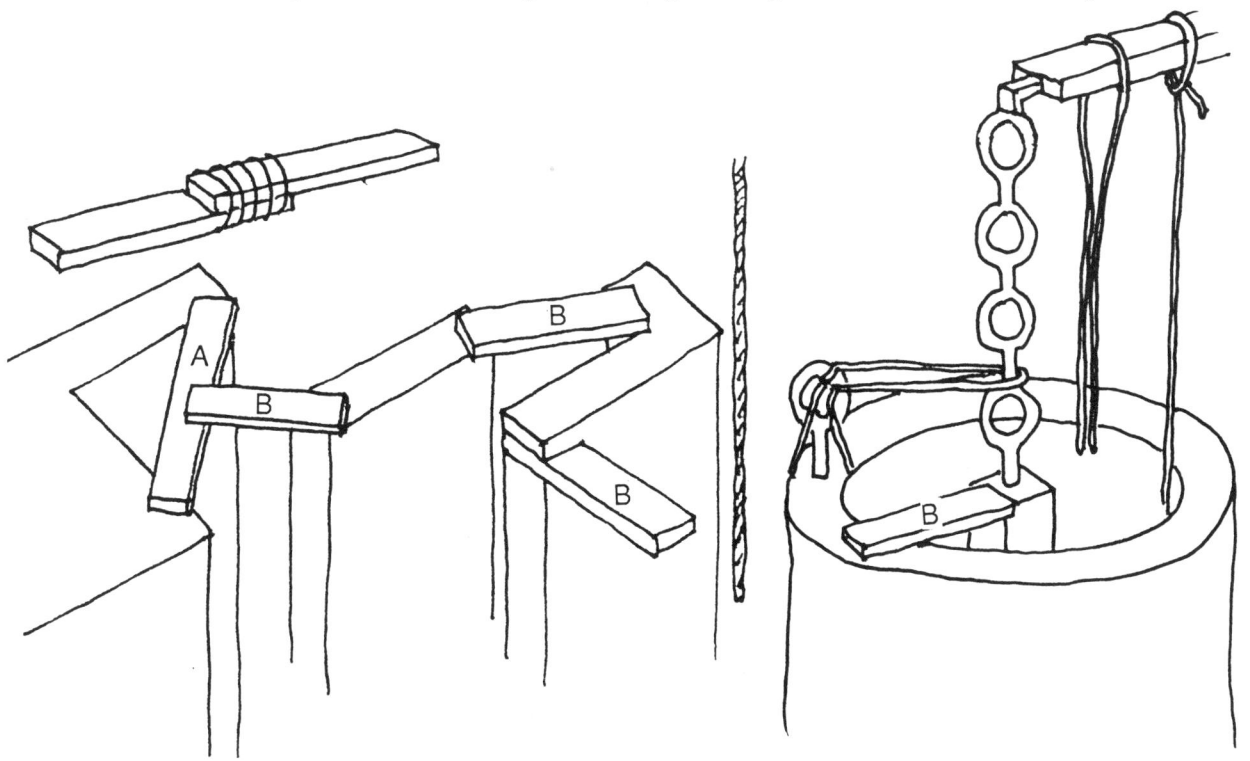

INITIATIVE TEST 4

It was very late and you were feeling very tired, so you pulled your caravan into a lay-by on a lonely country road. The vibration from driving along the bumpy roads had made the nine screws work loose on the side of the three hinges which held the door in position. As you opened the door of the caravan, all of the nine screws fell down the grate which you were parked against.

Write down and draw as many different solutions as you can to this problem.

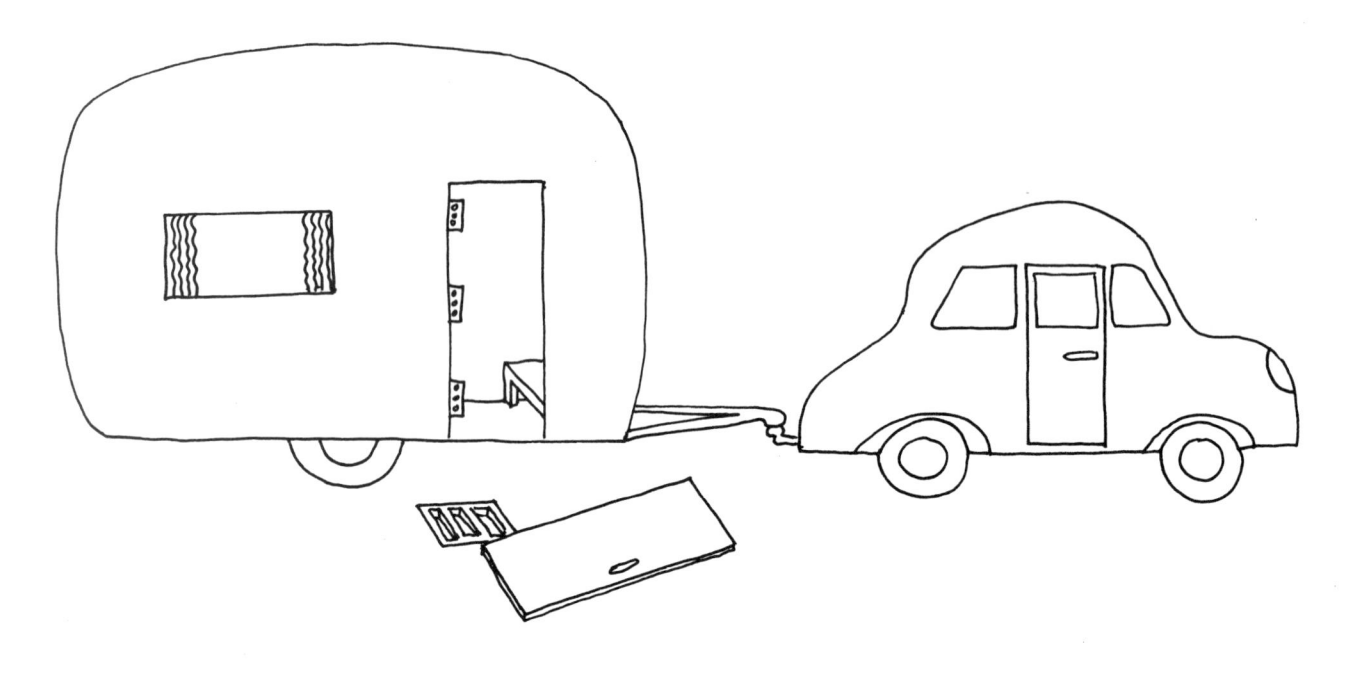

Some Possible Solutions

Can you find even more alternatives?

1. Travel without the door attached.
2. Tie it in position from the inside, then climb out of a window.
3. If the door will stay in position whilst the caravan is stationery, or can be tied in position from the inside, stay in the lay-by overnight. If the police arrive and want to move you, they will have to help you with the door.
4. Leave the caravan in the lay-by with the door in position and go for help.
5. Telephone the RAC or the AA or a 24-hour garage.
6. Try to retrieve screws from grate.
7. Remove one screw from each one of the hinges which are still attached to the caravan, or completely remove the middle hinge, or both. Then use the spare screws to temporarily hold the door in position.
8. Remove some screws from internal fitments.

An alternative to this initiative test is: You have a puncture in your car wheel and the wheel nuts fall down a drain. The nearest garage is ten miles away. You have no money and the traffic is very light. What can you do?

Some possible solutions are:

1. Remove drain top and try to reach them with sticks, magnet, etc.
2. Go for help.
3. Remove one wheel nut from each of the other wheels to attach the wheel back in position.

INITIATIVE TEST 5

The picture below shows a man in an isolated situation who is desperate for a drink of water.

The water can be seen falling through a small hole in the rock face. The maximum size of the hole is 200 mm in any direction and the falling water is just out of reach of the man's outstretched arm. The vertical rock face is smooth, with no hand or footholds to enable the man to reach the top of the spring.

Using graphics or text produce as many possible solutions as you can to the situation.

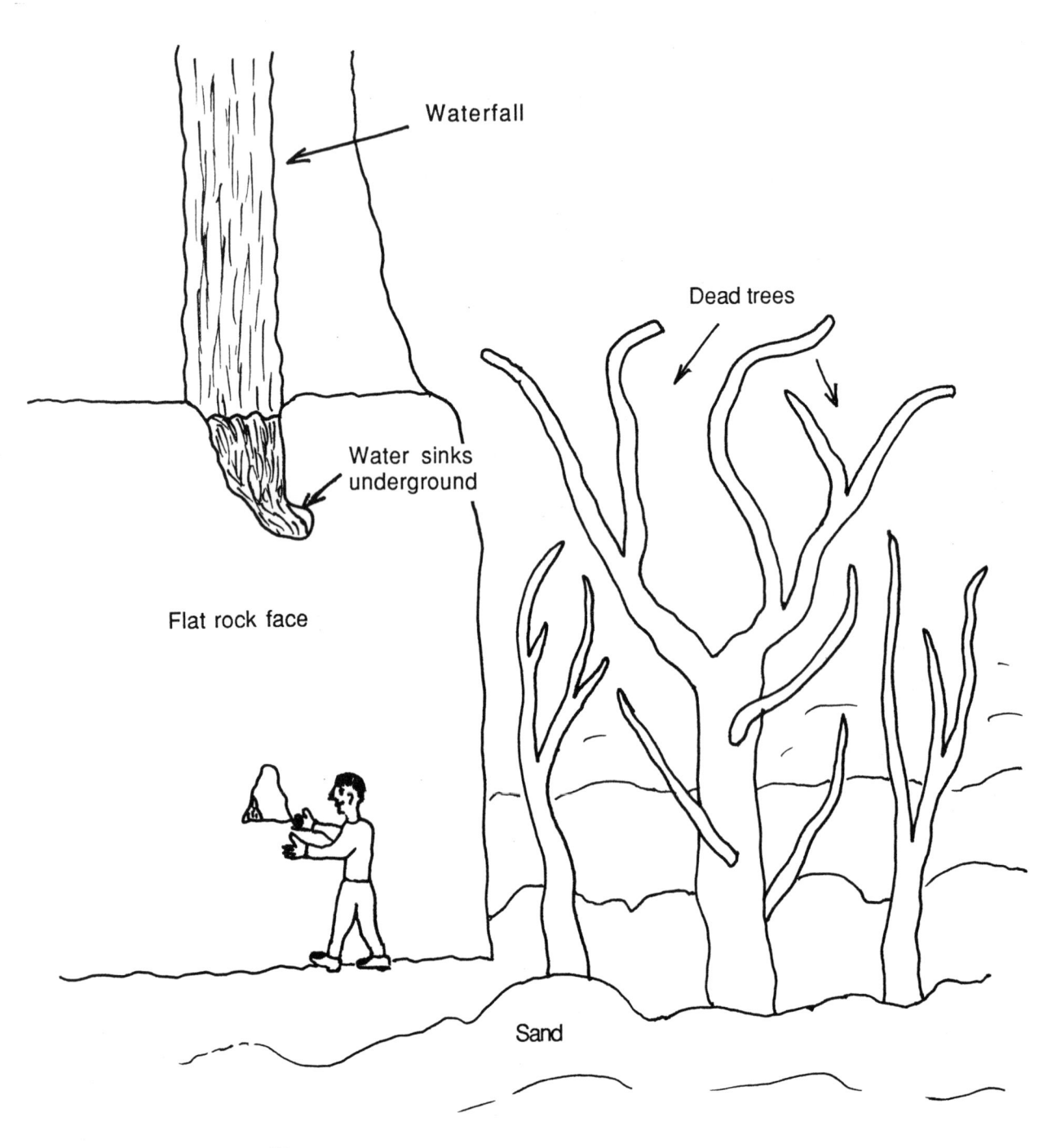

Waterfall

Dead trees

Water sinks underground

Flat rock face

Sand

Some Possible Solutions

Can you discover any more?

1. A stick placed at an angle would allow water to run down it and out of the hole.

2. Tie or wrap an article of clothing to a stick, using a shoe lace or the arms of a shirt or jumper, push it inside the triangular hole and allow the water to soak into the material. Then retrieve the clothing and squeeze out the water.

3. Use a stick to dig a hole in the sand to perhaps obtain moisture from the ground.

4. It may be possible to lean a long sturdy branch against the rock face and climb part of the way up, then use another branch with a curved or hooked end to attach it to the area where the water runs down the hole. This would then enable the man to pull himself to the top.

5. Throwing fairly large pieces of tree branch into the hole on top of the rock face may block it up sufficiently to cause some of the water to overflow down the front.

INITIATIVE TEST 6

The picture shows a man, hundreds of miles from civilisation. It is essential for him to cross the ravine. The sides of the very deep ravine, however, are smooth and vertical, and are impossible to climb down. The next nearest crossing point is over 50 miles away through dense jungle. If he went on this extra two- to three-day detour, he would arrive at his destination too late to save his daughter's life.

Using both graphics and text produce as many possible solutions as you can to the situation.

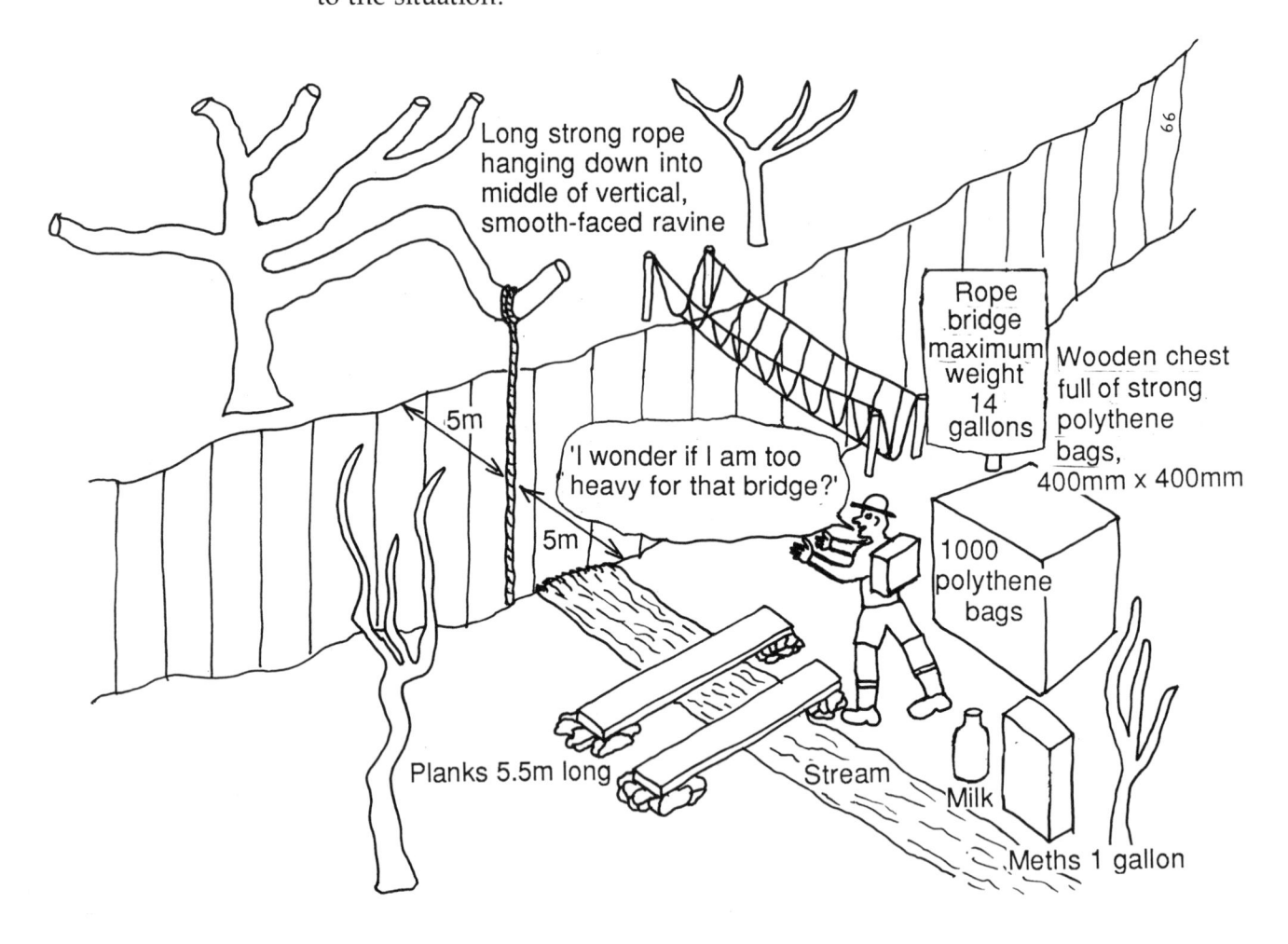

Some Possible Solutions

1. Throw back pack across and risk walking across.

2. Devise a method of weighing yourself with the available items to find out your gallon weight.

3. Tie together several polythene bags and use them as a rope to hold the two planks together, each overlapping the other by approximately 1 metre. Project the planks over the edge of the ravine until they almost touch the rope hanging down in the centre. Place the wooden chest on the planks near the opposite end to the rope and fill it with heavy rocks, or alternatively fill several polythene bags with water, tying up the tops, and place these inside the box. The weight would act as a counterbalance and enable you to walk out along the planks and then climb up the rope into the tree on the opposite side.

4. If the polythene bags are not strong enough to bind the two planks together, the same procedure could be used with a single plank but only projecting it 2½ metres over the edge. The rope would then have to be caught by using a long stick with an additional piece attached to the end, held in place by the polythene bags.

PART II

SUMMARY

This section is devoted to the principles of problem-solving.

The basic formula is the one provided by Professor K. F. Jackson in his book, *The Art of Solving Problems*. This has been slightly modified and given a simplified format. The complete process is shown overleaf.

During the following lessons each of the main stages is explained in detail with examples and exercises to practise each of them. Before the lessons begin there are answers to some awkward questions posed by students who have previously followed the course.

At the end of this section are two tests which cover the contents of the problem-solving process. A marking scheme is also available for each of them.

HOW TO SOLVE A PROBLEM

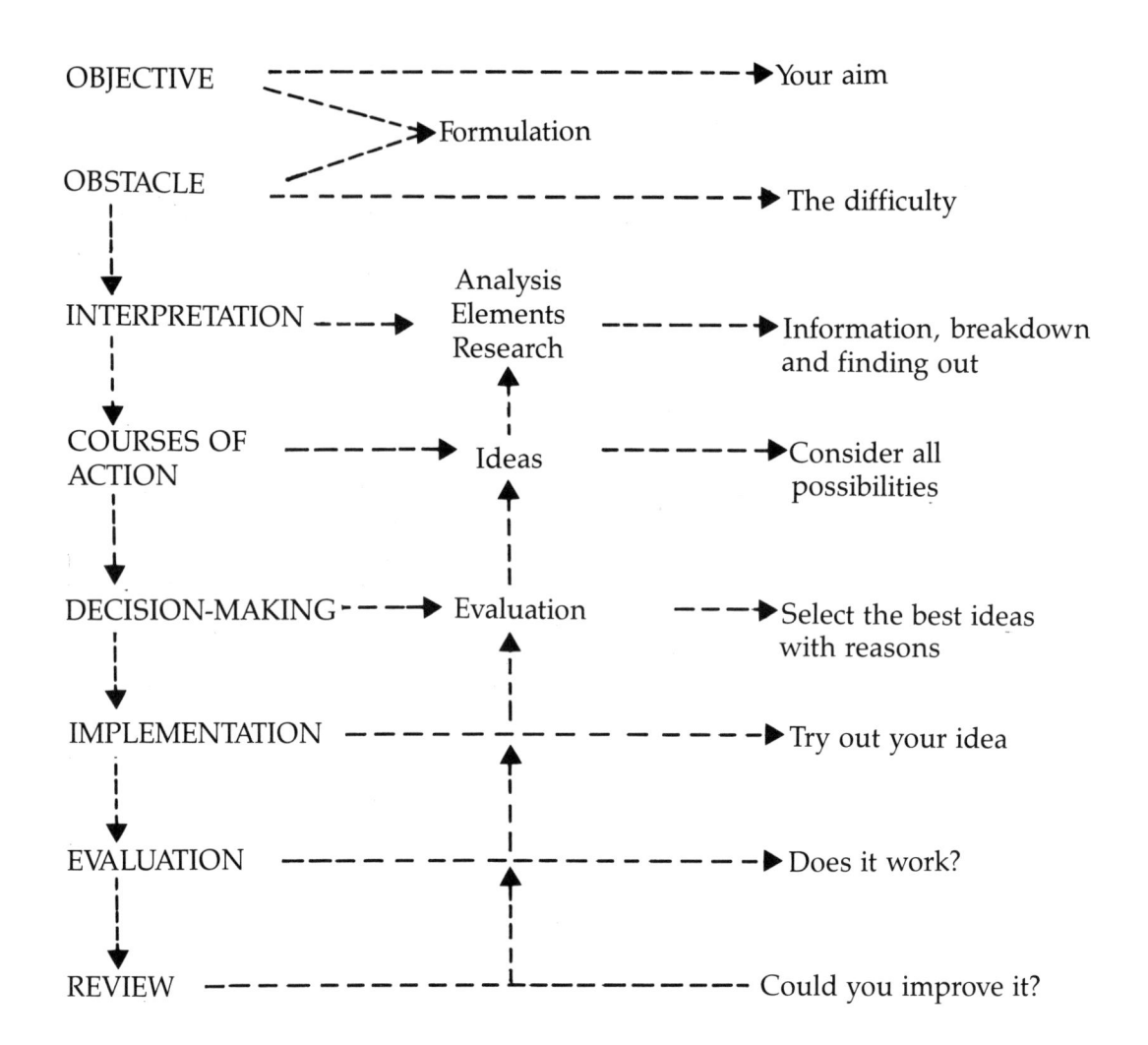

OBJECTIVE ---------→ Your aim

→ Formulation

OBSTACLE ---------→ The difficulty

↓

INTERPRETATION ---→ Analysis / Elements / Research ---→ Information, breakdown and finding out

↓

COURSES OF ACTION ---→ Ideas ---→ Consider all possibilities

↓

DECISION-MAKING ---→ Evaluation ---→ Select the best ideas with reasons

↓

IMPLEMENTATION ----------→ Try out your idea

↓

EVALUATION ----------→ Does it work?

↓

REVIEW ----------→ Could you improve it?

ANSWERS TO QUESTIONS ABOUT PROBLEM-SOLVING

1. *What is a problem?*

It is a difficult situation that possesses two features: an objective and an obstacle. Without both features, it is merely a task. However, even a task can be better tackled with developed thinking skills.

2. *Why does one need to be able to solve problems?*

Life is full of problems and the better one becomes at solving problems, the more one can control them or even prevent them from occurring because of an understanding of their cause.

3. *How can one deal with problems?*

Careful planning can prevent problems from occurring, but when one is faced with an objective plus an obstacle it is useful to have a methodical approach, such as the one developed by Professor K. Jackson and used in the second section of this book.

4. *Does one need to solve problems?*

The quality of life is dependent upon the number and difficulty of the problems one has to face. The strain and stress of a life full of unsolved difficulties must be avoided. One never reaches a stage where there are no problems to deal with, but the inability to solve them would lead to an intolerable situation.

5. *Does one need to improve one's ability to solve problems?*

As stated above, the better one is at solving problems, the better the quality of life. This is due to a clearer understanding of the causes of problems and an awareness of the various strategies which will overcome problems.

6. *Can one solve problems without this course?*

Some simple problems can be solved very easily, but more complex problems need a more developed skill and a wider understanding of their causes.

7. *Can one solve problems well without this course?*

Although an untrained problem-solver can produce acceptable courses of action to deal with simple problems, a trained problem-solver will produce many more alternatives and perhaps have a better chance of producing a more appropriate solution.

8. *Does normal, traditional subject teaching help us to solve problems?*

Teaching is often more concerned with 'content', with less attention paid to the thought process, and it is an unfortunate fact that the present formal examination system necessitates the assimilation of facts, rather than the process of thought, to guarantee good results.

Most teachers and educationalists, in stating their aims, say that their work is to teach pupils to think for themselves, rather implying that thinking is a by-product of learning. Not many would admit otherwise, because to put the emphasis on the thought process would mean altering the entire system.

Subject teachers would claim that in learning about their specialist area, a pupil would be forced to think. This is correct, but does thinking about something develop any transferable skill?

A sounder educational philosophy would be to develop skills in thinking as the chief aim, rather than merely filling our minds with facts. In other words, traditional subject teaching does not develop thinking skills in a way which is diverse enough to be of much use later in life. Edward de Bono says (1973);

> 'The old idea that skill in thinking would be developed as the by-product of attention to specific areas such as Geography and History is no longer tenable. Some thinking skills concerned with the sorting of information can be taught as a by-product of such subjects but these are only part of the broad range of thinking skills required in life.'

and:

> 'One advantage of developing thinking skill directly (as a specific subject) is that the skill can be applied to any situation since it has not been developed in a specific knowledge area.'

9. *Can we improve our ability to solve problems?*

Yes, we can. Problem-solving is better tackled if our ability to think is developed. Thinking is a skill, and like all skills, the more we practise, the better we will become at it. An awareness of all the different thinking strategies and an ability to use them, having practised them in cross-curricular situations, can not only improve our ability to solve problems but prevent them from occurring in the first place because of having a clearer understanding of their causes.

10. *Will improving my ability to solve problems help me at all?*

See Nos. 2, 4, 5 and 11.

11. *Will problem-solving improve my job prospects?*

One of the main qualities an employer looks for in his employees is the ability for them to think for themselves: the need for them to be able to tackle jobs using their own initiative and, when problems arise, to be able to deal with them without constantly needing the attention of others. Therefore, any qualifications or experience in the area of thinking for oneself can only be an advantage.

The ability to think will also help with organisation and gives additional confidence and a wider viewpoint, thus enabling one to work out more strategies for gaining employment.

12. *Will problem-solving help me in other subject areas?*

The ability to think for oneself will help in any area where difficulties arise.

Once a student has an understanding of problem-solving skills and a well-practised system, he or she is as well equipped as anyone can be for tackling any problem situation in any subject area. However, the application of the individual subject content to the conclusion of the problem and its success will depend upon other factors which may not be part of the initial thinking process.

13. *Will it help me later in life?*

Yes. See Nos. 2, 4, 5 and 11.

14. *Is there only one process or technique to develop skills in problem-solving?*

No. The process used here is to develop problem-solving skills and increase the number and variety of ways of tackling difficult situations. It should also make students aware of the wide variety of 'correct' answers there can be to a problem. Therefore, to say that there is only one way to develop problem-solving skills would be going against one of the main principles of this course. In fact, by the end of this course, both teachers and students should have developed their thinking skills enough to be able to produce a different course in developing problem-solving, which could be even better than this one! In other words, if this course in the development of the fluency of ideas works on the reader, it could be self-destructive.

15. *Will I be able to survive in life without being taught problem-solving?*

As there are various levels of achievement in other areas, such as Mathematics or English, there are various levels in problem-solving. Some people can barely read and write, or tackle simple mathematical problems such as adding up grocery bills. These people survive, but think how much better they would be, and more confident to enjoy life to the full, if they had developed their English and Mathematics to a higher level.

Most of us are stuck at the very basic stage in thinking skills, yet will survive, but advancement to a higher level can only improve our lifestyles. Edward de Bono says (1973) about being taught problem-solving that:

> 'The first point to be considered is whether thinking is natural or something that must be taught. Obviously, some thinking is natural, otherwise people would never be able to cope with everyday situations. But what about the situations with which people are not familiar? For instance, choosing a career is not a situation a pupil will be familiar with through everyday practice. The purpose of developing thinking as a deliberate skill is to enable a person to apply his skill to new and unfamiliar situations which have to be faced.'

16. *Can the problem-solving process be useful in any other areas?*

Many of us class certain situations as problems when they are merely tasks; for example, a pile of dirty plates, or an untidy garden are frequently referred to as 'problems'. In normal circumstances, both of the above situations would not have any obstacles involved to prevent the objectives from being achieved – therefore they should be regarded as tasks. They could become problems if normal circumstances were changed; for example, there may be no hot water available in which to wash the plates, or you may not possess any gardening equipment to help you tidy the garden.

Another area where the term 'problem-solving' has frequent usage is Mathematics; however, once again, unless we are without the appropriate knowledge to answer the questions, they should be referred to as 'tasks'. All this, however, does not make the problem-solving process any less useful in task situations. It merely means that there is no 'formulation' stage, but the remaining sequence of actions can prove to be very useful in helping one to understand thus overcoming the task in a way which may be more favourable than was originally anticipated.

The design process also benefits greatly from the problem-solving process in that it develops creativity. This will be considered later, in Part III.

LESSON 10: FORMULATING A PROBLEM – OBJECTIVES

Objective

To give the students an understanding of the formulation of a problem and how it can be broken down and clarified, concentrating on the objectives.

Resources

Exercise books

Content

Clarify what is meant by a problem, that is, P = O + O (Problem = Objective + Obstacle).

Look at examples of situations where people may be trying to achieve, change or avoid something, and ask the students to try to identify the objective or objectives in each one of them.

Ask the students to produce clear examples of the above objectives in sentence form, with maximum qualification, using a selection of given words; for example, bed, cow, tree, table, tape recorder.

Assignment

Give the group several more words to produce sentences which state precise objectives; e.g. piano, horse, rubber gloves, pen, hammer.

Teacher Notes

We all possess some ability to solve problems, but we can improve our skill in this area if we develop our thinking techniques. An awareness of all the different thinking strategies with regular practice, can not only improve our ability to solve problems but also prevent them from occurring. This is because we then have a clearer understanding of some of their causes. The ability to think develops additional confidence and a wider viewpoint, thus giving one an awareness of various strategies to overcome problems.

What is a problem? Professor K. Jackson (1983) says that 'A problem is a kind of difficult situation,' and, 'I am merely saying that all problems possess the two features I have just mentioned – an objective and an obstacle.'

Edward de Bono (1970) defines a problem by saying, 'A problem is simply the difference between what one has and what one wants,' and, 'In any problem there is a desired end point – something one wants to bring about. What one wants to bring about may take a variety of forms:

1. To resolve some difficulty (traffic congestion problem).
2. To bring about something new (design an apple-picking machine).
3. To do away with something unsatisfactory (road accidents, starvation).'

Both of the above named authors appear to agree that a problem has two components, one of them being the 'objective' or 'what one wants'. They do not, however, appear to agree on the second component. I have chosen to adopt Professor K. Jackson's definition, because during stage two of his suggested five stages of problem-solving, he considers the elements in the situation. This is the same as the first component in Edward de Bono's definition of a problem, 'what one has'. This means that the process used by Professor K. Jackson covers Edward de Bono's areas of consideration and more besides. Also, in the first instance, having a simple methodical approach to problem-solving can be advantageous when trying to teach and develop thinking skills. Once a thorough understanding of a sequence of operations has been established, then further and more specific methods can be applied at appropriate times. In a more recent publication, Hank Kahney (1986) states 'Any action taken by a person in pursuit of a blocked goal, whether physical or mental, is regarded as problem solving.' This definition also agrees with the formulation stage in Professor K. Jackson's problem-solving process (1983) 'Simply to state what the objective and the obstacle are is sufficient definition for any problem.'

The first stage in the problem-solving process, 'formulation', can be more easily remembered by the mnemonic $P = O + O$, where P is the problem and $O + O$ is the objective plus the obstacle.

The full problem-solving process is shown at the beginning of this section.

Ask the students to try to define the objectives of the people in the following situations:

1. A man is seen running in the direction of the railway station.

2. A group of people, with binoculars, are standing on the sea cliffs looking over the edge.

3. Two boys are dipping their fishing nets into a stream which runs along the edge of the golf course.

4. A blind man is waiting at the side of the road.

5. The farmer's wife is walking in the direction of the hen house with a basket in her hand.

It may be found that the objectives in each situation vary from student to student. If not, students should be asked to find alternative objectives to each of the situations. Because it is possible to produce alternative objectives to the above situations, it means they are ill-defined and consequently one can be led towards incorrect assumptions.

> 'In well-defined problems the solver is provided with four different sorts of information:
>
> 1. information about the initial state of the problem;
>
> 2. information about the goal state;
>
> 3. information about legal operators (things you are allowed to do in solving the problem);
>
> 4. information about the operator restrictions which constrain the application of operators.'
>
> *Hank Kahney* (1986)

Objectives have to be clear or one can end up trying to solve the wrong problem.

Give the group an unclear objective, for example, 'blackberries', and ask them to write a sentence with blackberries as a clear objective. They need to decide whether to change, achieve, or avoid something. Some answers could be:

1. 'You want to pick some blackberries.'
2. 'You want some blackberries.'
3. 'You want to find some blackberries.'
4. 'You want to sell some blackberries.'
5. 'You do not want any blackberries.'

Then ask the students to make their objectives even clearer by giving them even more qualification. For example:

1. 'Tomorrow you want to pick 2lb of large, ripe, sweet, blackberries.'
2. 'You want 1lb of large, ripe, blackberries by 1 o'clock.'

Expression of quality, quantity, size and timing makes the objective much more precise and there is less doubt about what is required. Care should be taken at this stage not to alter the objective. For example, if you wrote 'you want 2lb of large, ripe, sweet, blackberries to make a pie,' the objective would have been changed to making a pie rather than obtaining blackberries.

Here is an example of a situation which has a definite objective, but if you ask the students to write down the objective you may find that they come up with the wrong answer.

You were about to drive into Leeds to visit your sister when a lorry pulled up outside your house and dumped a very large load of sand at the end of the drive. The sand was meant for your next door neighbour, but the driver had misread the address.

My experience of using the above example is that many students decide that the objective is to move the sand, rather than the correct aim which is to visit your sister. This is probably because they immediately see the obstacle as being the sand, and the brain tends to want to tackle this obstacle in some way in order to release the car. Therefore dealing with the sand suddenly springs out as being the objective.

Many problems need careful thought before attempting to try to solve them, especially in sorting out the real objectives and avoiding being blinded by other influences.

LESSON 11: FORMULATING A PROBLEM – OBSTACLES

Objective

To give the students a clear understanding of the identification of an obstacle in a problem, and the existing strategies that could be used to overcome it.

Resources

Exercise books

Content

Introduce the students to the concept of obstacles and how to identify them in particular situations.

Look at examples (see Teacher Notes).

Ask the students to construct problems by adding obstacles to the sentences that they produced from the last lesson's objectives.

Show that problems can have more than one obstacle.

Use a full class discussion to produce a list of strategies to overcome obstacles. Having a selection of varied problems can be useful to assist with this task.

Assignment

Read the following problem, then write a clear statement of the objective and obstacle, suggesting some possible courses of action which could be taken, using the various strategies produced above.

Problem

A man wants to go home early to discuss with an insurance man about taking out a life insurance policy. Unfortunately he has a meeting at work.

Teacher Notes

Give examples of sentences which contain both objectives and obstacles and point out that an obstacle is something which prevents the objective from being reached. For example: I was going to go to the shop on my bicycle, to buy some ice cream, but I have just discovered that my front tyre is punctured.

I have found, that by this stage, many students have still not fully understood the difference between an objective, an obstacle, and whether or not there is actually a problem. As I mentioned in the previous lesson, we are easily led by the circumstances and by responding too quickly to situations we often misinterpret them. Edward de Bono (1975) says, 'Whether we like it or not we apply our emotions to the results of our perceptions. If we apply our emotions almost immediately without doing any perceptual work (that is to say thinking) then we apply our emotions to prejudices, clichés and stereotypes.'

It is useful to have a selection of situations, some of which contain objectives only and others containing obstacles only, to further develop the understanding of the students by questioning them individually. For example, ask the students to decide if the following are problems and, if they are not, to make them into problems by adding either an objective or an obstacle.

1. My dress is torn.
2. I want to go for a walk at 6 o'clock.
3. We were going to the pub at lunchtime.
4. I want to go for a swim in the sea this afternoon.
5. My front tyre is flat.
6. My car battery is flat.

Some students, when asked to decide upon the status of the above situations, will invariably see numbers 1, 5 and 6 as problems rather than obstacles. Emphasise that they do not become problems until an objective is added. Similarly, numbers 2, 3 and 4 require an obstacle adding to make them into problems. For example, in the first situation, the fact that your dress is torn does not present a problem until you need to wear it to go out somewhere.

Using the clear objectives produced during the last lesson, make more problem situations by adding an obstacle to each of them.

Another point which should be explored at this stage is that a problem can contain more than one obstacle. For example, you would like to go immediately to the shop to buy one litre of vanilla ice cream. The local shop is three miles away and there is a puncture in the front tyre of your bicycle, and you have also lost your money. The two obstacles in this situation are the flat tyre and the loss of your money. Both of these obstacles must be overcome in some way to achieve the final objective, which is to obtain some ice cream. Alternatively, modification of the objective could solve the problem.

Here are some examples of problems which may be useful in helping the students to discover various strategies to deal with problems.

1. Look at the situation we considered last lesson about your neighbour's load of sand being accidentally tipped at the end of your driveway when you were about to drive to your sister's house.
2. You want to open the top window but there is a desk in the way approximately sixty centimetres away from the window ledge.
3. You would like to grow some alkaline loving plants but your soil is acidic.
4. You have to cross over a very high, narrow, rope bridge but you are afraid of heights.
5. You would like to expand your business but the owner of the next field is objecting to it.
6. You were driving along a narrow country road, in your car, when you came to a rut across the road which was a little too deep for the car wheels to pass over without damaging the base of the car. You need to arrive at your destination with the vehicle in good condition, and you do not have enough time to turn around and follow an alternative route.

7. You want to break open the shell of a walnut but the device you have to use can exert only a small amount of pressure.

8. You were on the way to visit your sister when the river overflowed and blocked all the roads into the village where she lives.

List of Possible Strategies

Turn it to your advantage.
Take it away or have it removed.
Destroy it.
Prove that an obstacle does not really exist.
Be patient and it may go away.
Bribe it in some way.
Modify it.
Discover a weak area.
Avoid it.
Go around it.
Go under it or tunnel.
Bridge it or go over it.
Neutralise it.
Overcome it.

> 'By now it should be perfectly clear what kind of ideas we are looking for because the whole purpose of considering the timing, outcome, objective and obstacle strategically is to bring into focus the issues which really matter.'
>
> K. F. Jackson (1975)

Possible Solutions to the Assignment

Objective – To find out about a life insurance policy

Obstacle – Meeting at work

Possible courses of action

1. Postpone meeting.
2. Deal with it by telephone.
3. Change the time of the meeting at work.
4. Be late for insurance man.
5. Tell the insurance man to come another evening.
6. Ask the insurance man to come to work.
7. Ask if someone could deputise for you at the meeting.
8. Ask someone else to talk to the insurance man and report back to you.

LESSON 12: INTERPRETING A PROBLEM

Objective

To give a clear understanding of the interpretation or investigation stage and how to use it to develop our thinking skills.

Resources

Exercise books
Screwdriver
Torch
Sports bag

Content

Introduce the students to the term 'interpretation' (investigation).

Show the various stages of interpretation, that is:

1. breaking down the situation into its elements;
2. analysing each element;
3. analysing relationships between the elements;
4. researching the information gained from the analysis.

Ask the students to write down a list of elements for each of the following items:

Screwdriver
Torch
Sports bag

Any other items may be used.

From a given problem, ask the students to 'formulate' it, produce a list of elements, then analyse and research them.

Assignment

Ask the students to select any three items and make a list of the major elements in each one.

Teacher Notes

We have now established a logical process to define a problem and give a clear direction and possible strategies to deal with it. In order to further stimulate divergent and numerous ideas to give us a better chance of finding the most 'appropriate' solution to a problem, we now need to 'interpret' or 'investigate' the situation.

As the 'formulation' can itself be broken down into stages, so can 'interpretation'. These stages are:

1. Elements and relationships between them.
2. Analysis – asking questions about the elements.
3. Research – finding out the answers to the above questions.

Elements

I have found that this term can cause some confusion because of its many different applications. To further add to the confusion, an element itself may be broken down into smaller elements.

To try to explain what I mean when I ask students to list the major elements in an article, I will give examples using the items mentioned in the content notes on the previous page.

1. *Screwdriver* – handle, shaft and blade.

2. *Torch* – container, batteries, bulb, reflector, switch, lens, fastenings and fitments.

3. *Sports bag* – container, handle, compartments, fastenings and fitments.

It should be noted that plastic, wood, metal, chrome, etc. are not included as major elements of a screwdriver. They are elements of the major elements. Similarly, the bulb is a major element of a torch, but the glass bulb, the filament, the screw or bayonet fitment and the metals are elements of the bulb.

Breaking an item down into its elements is a very useful process when trying to stimulate the imagination into producing new designs. It helps the mind to break away from visualising only completed ready-made products and gives the opportunity for creativity. This technique will be mentioned in more detail in the design section later in this book.

It is far more difficult to extract the major elements from a situation than it is from an object. Here is an example of a situation, and most of the major elements have been extracted and listed below it.

Problem

A married couple have four sons who work away from home and often go back to stay for a few days, but not always at the same time.

None of the sons can give more than one day's notice, usually much less, that they will be arriving and this creates the problem of not knowing how much milk to order each day.

Formulation

Objective: To have enough milk for everyone.

Obstacle: The number of people requiring milk can vary from day to day with very little warning.

Interpretation

Elements

1. The sons
2. The parents
3. The milk
4. One day's notice

5. Work
6. Work location
7. Milkman
8. The home and surroundings
9. Time
10. The journey from work to parents

Element   *Information Sought* (analysis)

1. The sons   Is milk available where each son works?
                             Is milk available in the area where each son lives?
                             Do they all want milk?
                             Do they all have a preference for fresh milk?

2. The parents   Do the parents always keep extra milk?
                             Have they got a fridge?
                             Are they bothered about going without milk themselves?

3. The milk   From where is milk obtained?
                             Which different types of milk are available?
                             Do they all taste the same?
                             Could the flavour be altered?
                             Are there any alternatives to milk?
                             Could the milk be diluted?

4. One day's notice   Is one day's notice enough time to buy or order extra milk?
                             Do the sons always give a full day's notice?

5. Work   Can milk be obtained from work?
                             Could they be allowed out of work to buy milk ready for the journey?

6. Work location   Are there any shops in the area where each son works?
                             Do they sell milk?
                             If there are some shops which sell milk, are they always open at the time the sons start their journey?
                             Do they ever run out of milk?
                             Can milk be obtained anywhere else locally? e.g. farm, dairy, friends.

7. Milkman   Does the milkman deliver every day?
                             Does he always carry spare milk with him on his rounds?
                             Does he ever run out of milk?
                             Does he live locally?
                             Could milk be obtained from him by calling at his house?
                             What time does he deliver the milk?
                             Can he be contacted by telephone?

8. The parents' home   Is there always plenty of milk in the house?
   and surroundings   Are there any alternatives to fresh milk in the house? e.g. Powdered milk, U.H.T., evaporated.

		Could milk be obtained from local shops?
		Are there any local shops which stay open late?
		Do they stock milk?
		Do they ever run out of milk?
		Are there any neighbours?
		Are they friendly enough to lend you milk?
		Are there any milk-producing animals in the area?
		Is there a farm or dairy in the area?
9.	Time	What time do the sons usually arrive?
		Do they require milk at the time they arrive?
10.	The journey from work to parents	Which mode of transport do the sons use?
		Could they stop off somewhere on the journey to obtain milk?

The third stage of interpretation is 'research'. All the above analysis needs further investigation. The combination of isolating the elements, analysing and researching them, helps to generate many ideas and allows one to pursue other avenues which may have gone unnoticed without this stage.

Some possible courses of action which have been generated by the above analysis, without the research, are:

For the sons to: not bother
bring milk from where they live or work
buy some on the journey
go without milk
not to visit unless they have obtained milk.

For the parents to: go without milk and give it to sons
borrow some
inform the milkman in time
not bother about the sons having milk
find an alternative to milk
go to the dairy
go to the farm
keep cows or goats
keep in extra milk at all times
keep in extra long-life milk (U.H.T., evaporated milk)
keep powdered milk
buy some from the shops if notified before they close
buy some from the 'Off Licence'
tell the sons not to expect any milk if they do not give you more notice
find a milk substitute.

By the time the students have completed the analysis stage in the above problem, with assistance, and can visualise the volume of work now required to research all of the analysis, they will probably question the length of time that needs to be spent on a simple problem. Generally speaking, most students are in a great hurry and since the majority of students could produce a quick 'adequate' solution to most situations, they will find spending additional time thinking as a waste of time. However, at this stage it must be re-enforced that the development of thinking skills depends on slowing down the decision-making process a little and giving more time to the exploratory stages. This includes considering areas which would normally be regarded as silly or not applicable. This matter was dealt with earlier in Lessons 6 and 7.

> 'The majority of pupils will not enjoy thinking. Very few people do. Thinking is frustrating because by definition its purpose is to achieve something that cannot be achieved without thinking . . . Left to themselves, pupils would prefer not to think, but to answer from 'stock' just as a shop assistant would rather hand you something off the shelf than have to order it . . . Teachers should not be discouraged if pupils say they do not like thinking or find the lessons 'boring'. This is natural and in time it wears off.'
>
> *Edward de Bono* (1973)

LESSON 13: INVESTIGATION, USING TOPIC WEBS

Objective

To make students aware of an alternative method of recording information. In this case laying out information in the form of a topic web.

Resources

Exercise books

Content

Use the following situation to give the students experience in the use of the topic web display technique in analysing, researching and evaluating.

Problem: The Meals on a Duke of Edinburgh Award Expedition (Bronze Level)

You are one of a party of four people about to embark upon a Bronze Duke of Edinburgh Award Expedition.

You have volunteered to be responsible for planning the meals and buying the food.

The total amount of food and equipment will be shared out and carried between the four participants.

The Bronze expedition lasts two days, including one night away from home, camping, and the minimum distance to be covered during the two days is 15 miles. This distance must be covered by foot. There is also a minimum time of 12 hours' planned activity (6 hours per day), which includes one hour for setting up and striking camp.

It is also a requirement that at least one substantial meal is cooked daily.

The food is normally carried by the participants but fresh produce may be purchased on the journey, and drinking water may be drawn from houses.

Interpretation

The two areas which need investigating are:

1. The types of meals possible with the constraints of the award eventually applied.
2. The content of each meal, with any constraints eventually applied, such as cost, weight, calorific value, nutritional value, taste, appearance, various dietary requirements, ease of preparation, cooking facilities available, time available.

Tackle investigation No. 1 as a shared class exercise (shown on page 80).

Students to work as individuals on the production of an investigation topic web of the hot breakfast. This can be followed by a topic web investigation of the cooked evening meal.

Produce a summary of the final choice of meals and content after each of the above topic webs.

Share answers and information at the end of the exercise.

Depending on the interest generated and the possibility that some of the students may be involved with the D. of E. scheme, it may be considered worthwhile continuing the exercise as a major project.

A worked example is given below, concluding with a shopping list, which would need pricing in order to inform the other three participants of their share of the cost.

Try to see which students can spend the least amount of money on food, but still remain above the minimum requirements of the award, and above the minimum food requirements needed for this type of exercise.

Assignment

In one of your subjects at school, the grades you receive are always very poor, and you would like to work out exactly why this occurs so that you can do something about it.

From the above problem produce a topic web investigation of the possibilities of what may be affecting your grades (the elements) including analysis of each element.

Teacher Notes

Below is an example of a possible topic web analysis of the given assignment.

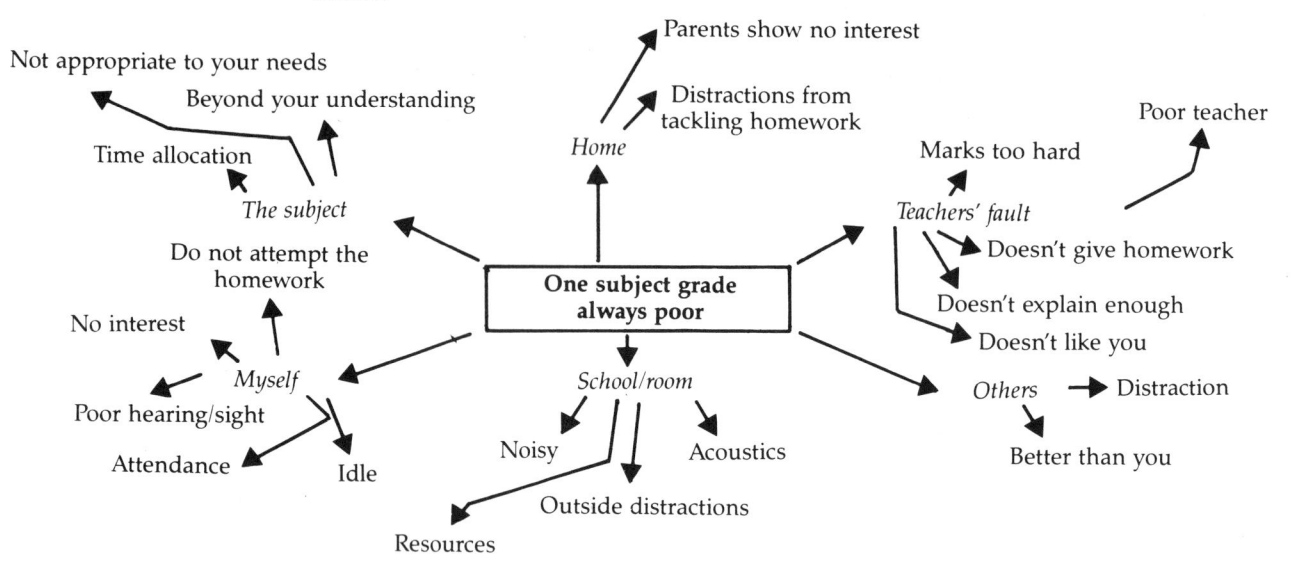

Not appropriate to your needs
Beyond your understanding
Time allocation
The subject
Do not attempt the homework
No interest
Myself
Poor hearing/sight
Attendance
Idle

One subject grade always poor

Parents show no interest
Distractions from tackling homework
Home
Marks too hard
Teachers' fault
Poor teacher
Doesn't give homework
Doesn't explain enough
Doesn't like you
Others → *Distraction*
Better than you
School/room
Noisy
Acoustics
Outside distractions
Resources

A Worked Example of the Meals on the Duke of Edinburgh Award Expedition

Formulation

Objective: To find out which meals are required
Obstacle: The requirements of the award

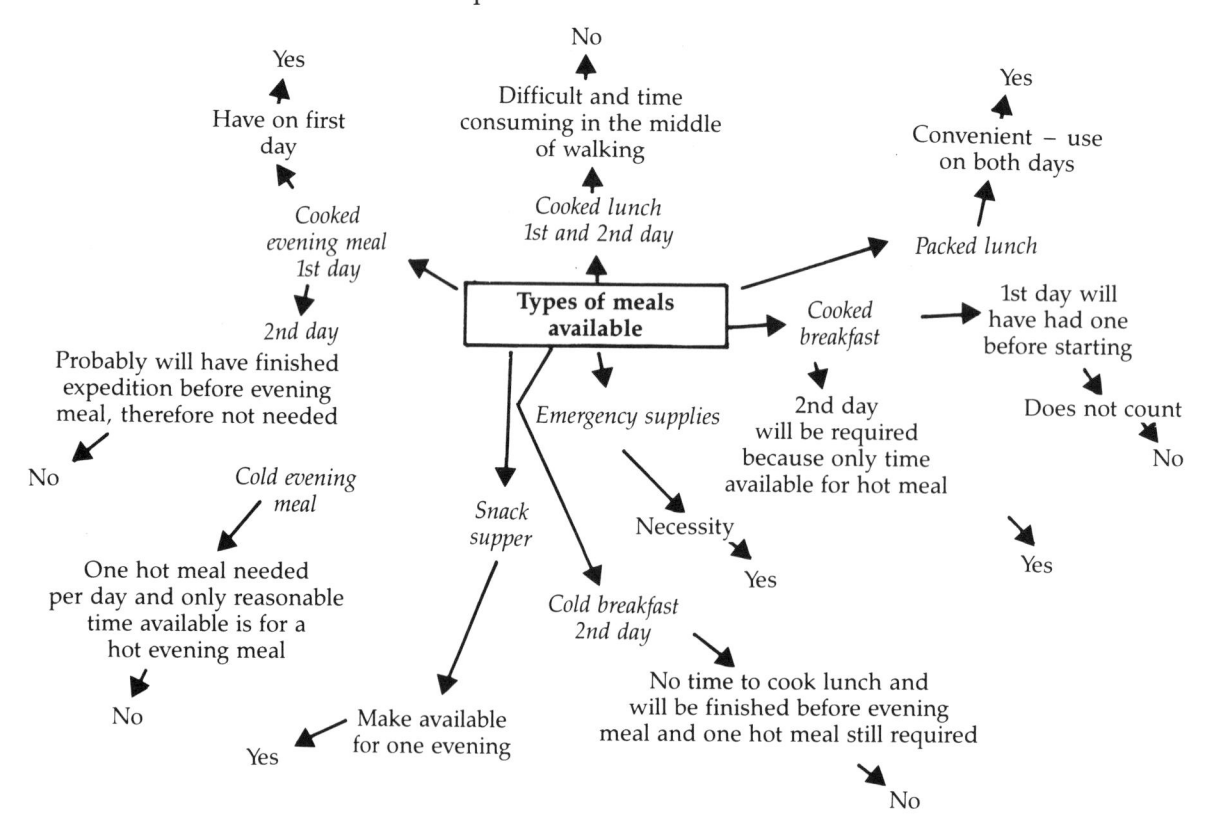

Yes
Have on first day
Cooked evening meal 1st day
2nd day
Probably will have finished expedition before evening meal, therefore not needed
No
Cold evening meal
One hot meal needed per day and only reasonable time available is for a hot evening meal
No

No
Difficult and time consuming in the middle of walking
Cooked lunch 1st and 2nd day

Types of meals available

Emergency supplies
Snack supper
Make available for one evening
Yes

Cold breakfast 2nd day
No time to cook lunch and will be finished before evening meal and one hot meal still required
No

Cooked breakfast
2nd day will be required because only time available for hot meal
Necessity
Yes

Yes
Convenient – use on both days
Packed lunch
1st day will have had one before starting
Does not count
No
Yes

Summary:
One hot breakfast needed (for four people).
One hot evening meal needed (for four people).
One snack supper but not essential (for four people).
Two packed lunches needed each (for four people).
Emergency supplies for four.

The meals

Analysis
What to eat at each meal?
Cost?
Convenience foods?
Weight to carry?
Volume per person?
Nutritional value?
Fresh supplies?
Minimum number of kcals required per meal/day?
Taste/diets?
Time available?
Cooking facilities available?

Research
The cost of the food should be kept as low as possible.
It is advisable to use convenience food whenever possible, e.g. ready cooked, dried food, etc.
Avoid heavy packaging, such as tins, wherever possible.
When involved with strenuous walking, a minimum food intake of 2700 kcals per day is recommended: approximately 900 kcals per meal.
Fresh produce can be obtained on route, including drinking water. Examples of fresh produce which can be obtained are milk, eggs, meat, vegetables, etc.
What is the total maximum weight that each person should be carrying?
Emergency supplies should be carried and there should be enough to sustain each member of the group for at least one whole day.
What are the cooking facilities available?
No member of the group is following a special diet.

1. *Breakfast*

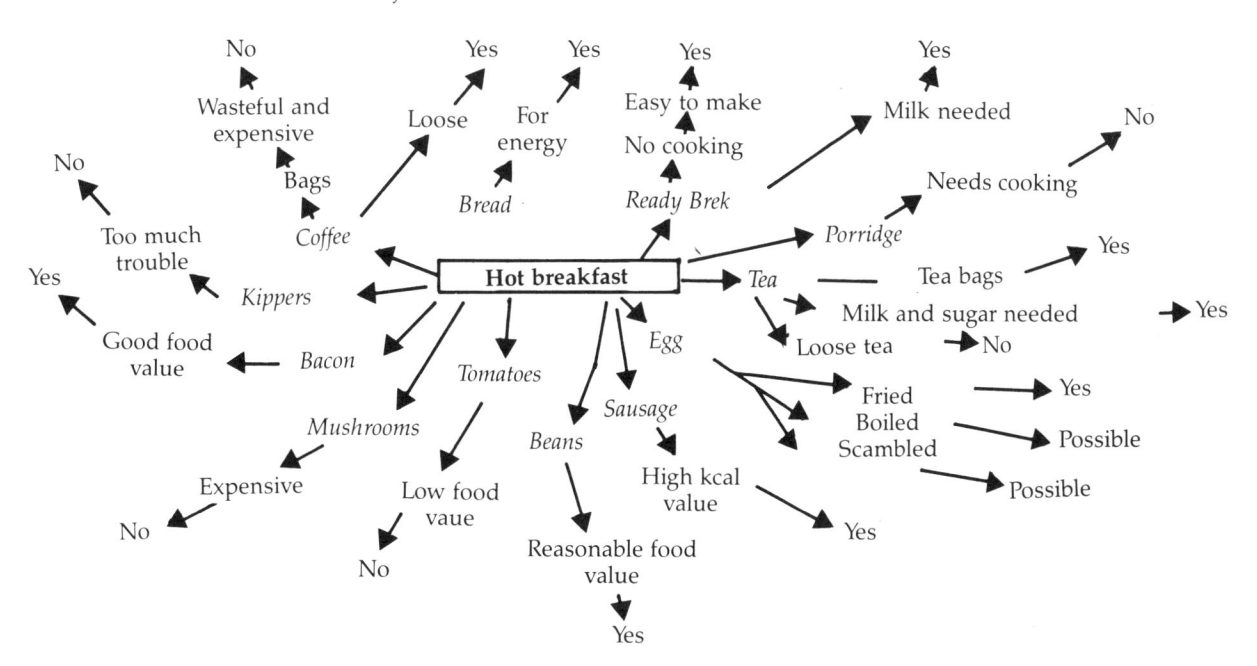

[Diagram: Hot breakfast branching to: Coffee (Bags → Loose → Yes; Wasteful and expensive → No), Kippers (Too much trouble → No), Bacon (Good food value → Yes), Mushrooms (Expensive → No), Tomatoes (Low food value → No), Beans (Reasonable food value → Yes), Sausage (High kcal value → Yes), Egg (Fried → Yes; Boiled → Possible; Scrambled → Possible), Bread (For energy → Yes), Ready Brek (Easy to make, No cooking → Yes; Milk needed → Yes), Porridge (Needs cooking → No), Tea (Tea bags → Yes; Loose tea → No; Milk and sugar needed → Yes)]

Summary: Ready Brek, milk, bacon, sausage, egg, beans, tea bags, loose coffee, milk for drinks, sugar, cooking oil, bread, margarine, salt. The milk and eggs will be bought from a local farm, just before pitching camp. This will be pre-arranged before the expedition.

2. Cooked Evening Meal

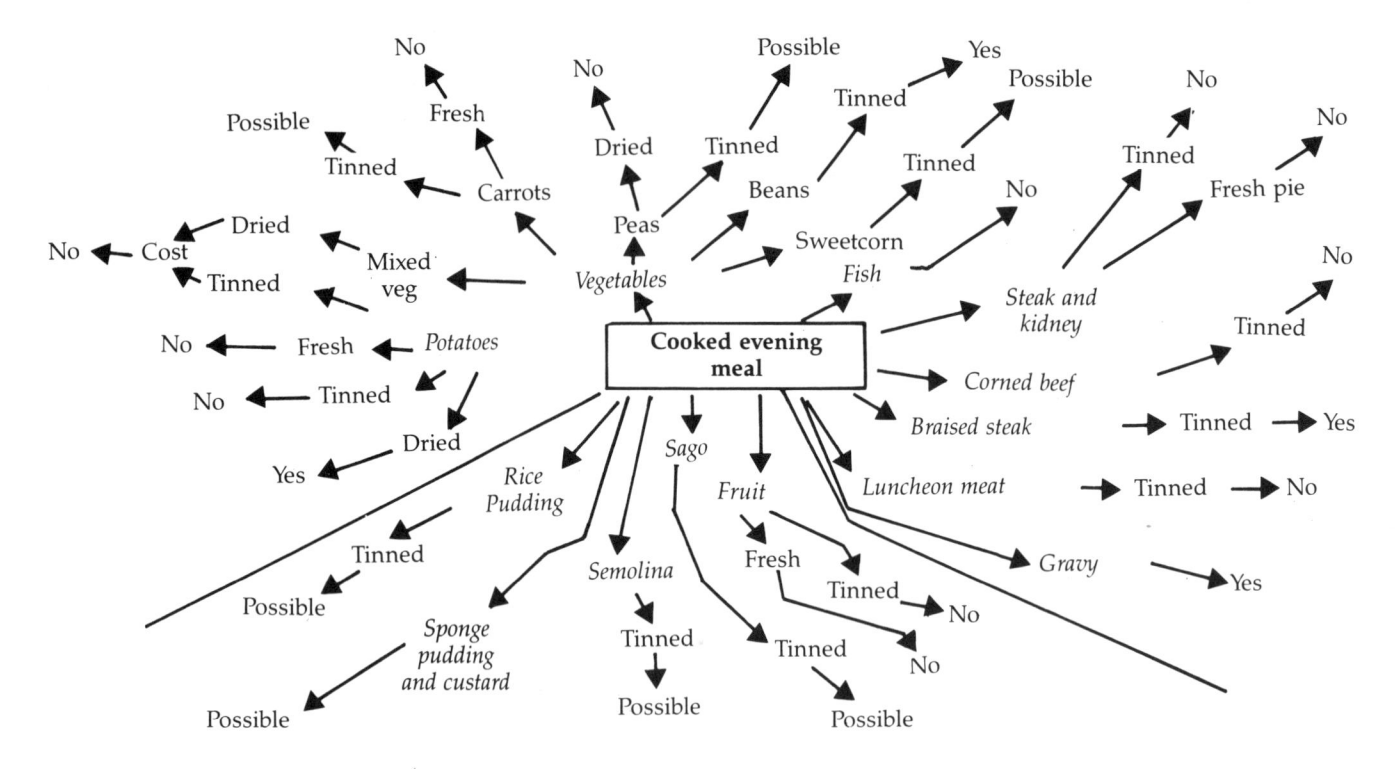

[Mind map diagram with "Cooked evening meal" at the center, branching to:]

- **Vegetables**: Potatoes (Fresh → No; Tinned → No; Dried → Yes), Mixed veg (Cost → No; Tinned → Possible; Dried → No), Carrots (Fresh → No; Tinned → Possible), Peas (Dried → No; Tinned → Possible), Beans (Tinned → Possible), Sweetcorn (Tinned → Yes; Tinned → Possible; No)
- **Fish**: No; Tinned → No
- **Steak and kidney**: Fresh pie → No; Tinned → No
- **Corned beef**: Tinned → No
- **Braised steak**: Tinned → Yes
- **Luncheon meat**: Tinned → No
- **Gravy**: Yes
- **Rice Pudding**: Tinned → Possible
- **Sago**: Tinned → Possible
- **Semolina**: Tinned → Possible
- **Fruit**: Fresh → No; Tinned → No
- **Sponge pudding and custard**: Possible

Summary: Braised steak (tinned), potatoes (dried), carrots (tinned), peas (tinned), rice pudding (tinned), salt, tea and coffee plus milk and sugar, margarine. (I would rather have the convenience and taste of tinned food and pay the forfeit of extra weight.)

3. Packed lunches

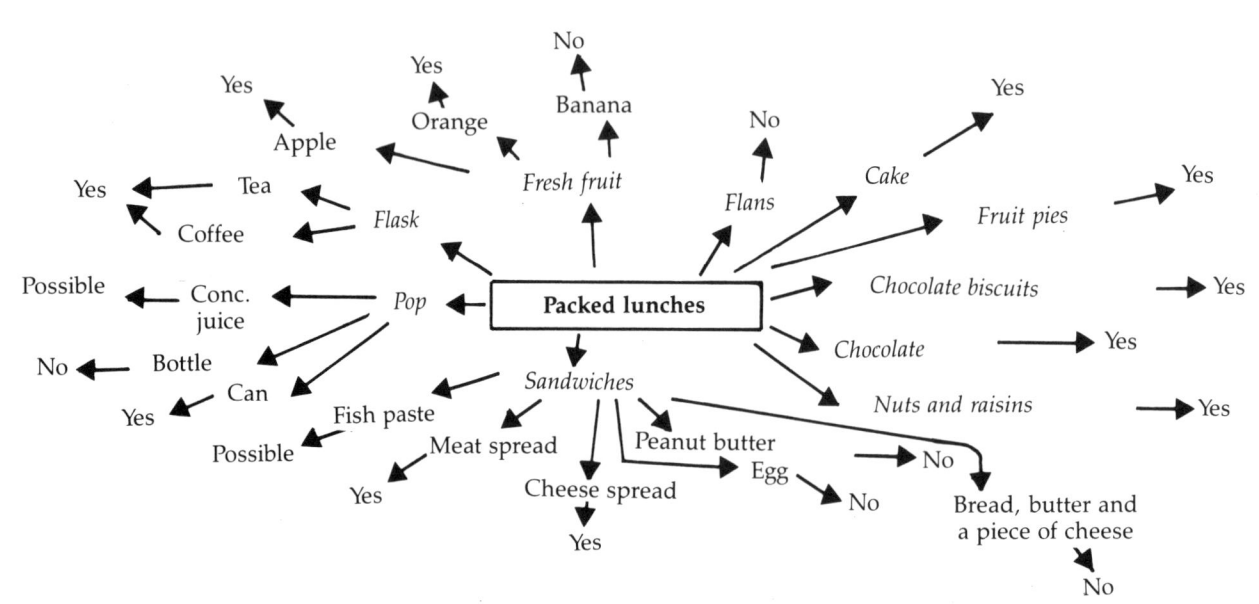

[Mind map diagram with "Packed lunches" at the center, branching to:]

- **Fresh fruit**: Apple → Yes; Orange → Yes; Banana → No
- **Flask**: Tea → Yes; Coffee → Yes
- **Pop**: Conc. juice → Possible; Bottle → No; Can → Yes
- **Sandwiches**: Fish paste → Possible; Meat spread → Yes; Cheese spread → Yes; Peanut butter → No; Egg → No
- **Flans**: No
- **Cake**: Yes
- **Fruit pies**: Yes
- **Chocolate biscuits**: Yes
- **Chocolate**: Yes
- **Nuts and raisins**: Yes
- **Bread, butter and a piece of cheese**: No

Summary – 1st packed lunch: Sandwiches (bread, butter/marg, cheese spread), nuts and raisins, chocolate, chocolate biscuits, fruit pie, can of pop, apple, flask of coffee, milk, sugar.

Summary – 2nd packed lunch: Sandwiches (bread, butter/marg, meat spread), nuts and raisins, chocolate biscuits, chocolate, cake, orange, can of pop, flask of tea, milk, sugar.

4. *Supper*

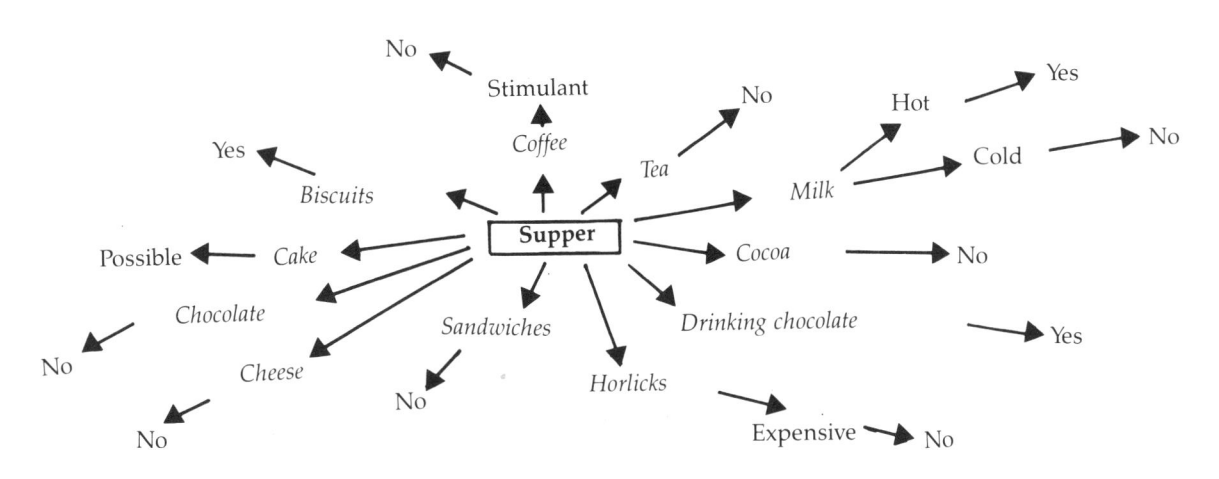

```
         No                              Yes
          ↖         No                    ↑
       Stimulant    ↑         Hot         ↑
          ↑        Tea         ↗         Cold ——→ No
  Yes    Coffee     ↑   Milk ——→
   ↖       ↑        ↑    ↘
   Biscuits ↑       ↑     Cocoa ——→ No
      ↖    ┌────────┐
Possible ← │ Supper │
   ← Cake  └────────┘
          ↙   ↓   ↘
   Chocolate  ↓    Drinking chocolate ——→ Yes
      ↙    Sandwiches  ↘
    No    ↙    ↓    Horlicks
       Cheese  No        ↘
        ↙              Expensive ——→ No
       No
```

Summary: Hot milk with drinking chocolate and biscuits.

5. *Emergency supplies*

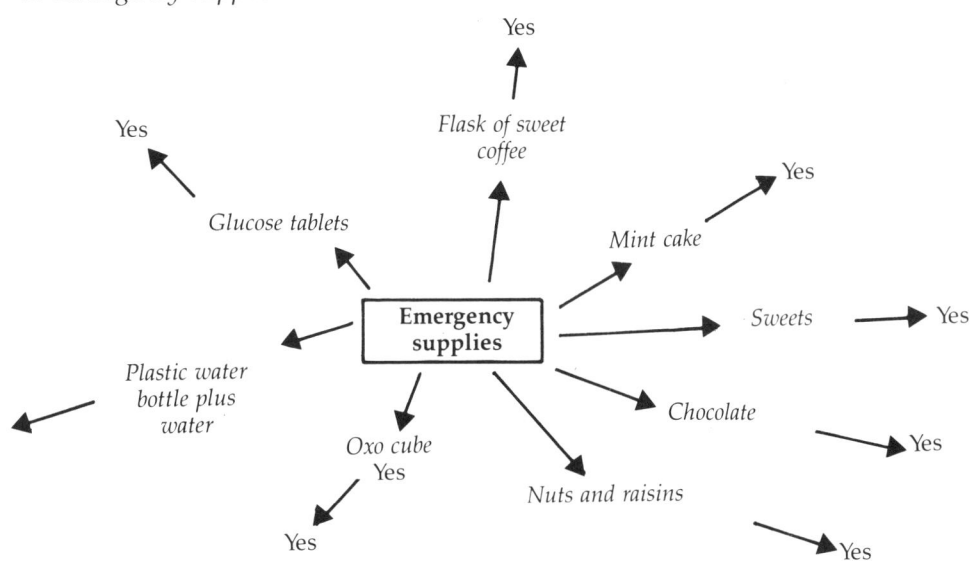

```
                    Yes
                     ↑
                Flask of sweet
                    coffee
   Yes                ↑                Yes
    ↖                 │                 ↗
   Glucose tablets    │        Mint cake
          ↖       ┌──────────┐    ↗
                  │Emergency │         Sweets ——→ Yes
                  │supplies  │
   Plastic water  └──────────┘    ↘
   bottle plus    ↙    ↓    ↘    Chocolate ——→ Yes
      water    Oxo cube   Nuts and raisins
               Yes                    ↘
                ↓                      Yes
               Yes
```

Summary: Glucose tablets, Kendal mint cake, chocolate, nuts and raisins, Oxo cube, water in a plastic bottle, flask of sweet coffee.

Development

1. *Hot Breakfast*	*Amount Per Person*	*Calorific Value*
Ready Brek	1 oz raw	100
Milk	½ pt	280
Bacon	2 oz (2 rashers)	220
Sausage	2 oz (2)	165
Egg (fried)	2 oz (1)	135
Baked beans	2 oz	50
Tea	2 tea bags	0
Coffee	2 spoonfuls	0
Bread	1 slice	70
Cooking oil	½ fl oz	0
Sugar	1 oz	110
Salt		0
		1130 Kcals

Summary of food needed for breakfast for four people:

Ready Brek	4 oz
Milk	2 pt
Bacon	8 oz
Sausage	8 oz
Eggs	4
Baked beans	8 oz
Tea	8 tea bags
Coffee	2 oz
Bread	4 slices
Cooking oil	2 fl oz
Sugar	4 oz
Salt	1 oz

2. *Evening Meal*	*Amount Per Person*	*Calorific Value*
Braised steak	4 oz	220
Potatoes	4 oz	90
Carrots	2 oz	10
Peas	4 oz	95
Rice pudding	6 oz	200
Tea	2 tea bags	0
Coffee	2 tsp	0
Milk	¼ pt	90
Sugar	½ oz	55
Margarine	1 oz	210
Salt		0
Gravy	¼ oz	0
		970 Kcals

Summary of food needed for evening meals for four people:

Braised steak	1 lb
Potatoes	1 lb
Carrots	8 oz
Peas	1 lb
Rice pudding	24 oz
Tea	8 tea bags
Coffee	2 oz
Milk	1 pt
Sugar	2 oz
Margarine	4 oz
Salt	
Gravy	1 oz

3. *Packed Lunch 1st Day*

	Amount Per Person	Calorific Value
Bread	2 slices	100
Margarine	½ oz	100
Cheese spread	2 small (2 oz)	200
Nuts and raisins	1 pkt	200
Chocolate biscuits	1 Penguin or similar	75
Chocolate	1 × 4 oz bar	600
Fruit pie	1 small pie	200
Can of pop	1 can	110
Apple	1	40
Coffee	2 tsp	0
Milk	¼ pt	0
Sugar	1 oz	110
		1825 Kcals

Packed Lunch 2nd Day

	Amount Per Person	Calorific Value
Bread	2 slices	100
Margarine	½ oz	100
Meat spread	2 oz	120
Nuts and raisins	1 packet	200
Chocolate biscuit	1 Penguin or similar	75
Cake	1 × 2 oz piece	200
Can of pop	1 can	110
Orange	1 × 4 oz	40
Tea	2 bags	0
Milk	¼ pt	90
Sugar	1 oz	110
Chocolate	1 × 4 oz bar	600
		1740 Kcals

Summary of both packed lunches for four people:

Bread	16 slices
Margarine	4 oz
Meat spread	8 oz
Cheese spread	8 oz
Nuts and raisins	8 pkts
Cake	4 pieces
Fruit pies	4
Coffee	6 oz
Tea	8 bags
Chocolate	8 × 4 oz
Chocolate biscuits	8
Can of pop	8
Apples	4
Oranges	4
Milk	2 pts
Sugar	8 oz

4. *Summary of Supper for Four People*

Milk	2 pkts
Plain biscuits	1 pkt
Sugar	2 oz
Drinking chocolate	2 oz

5. *Emergency Supplies for Four People*

Oxo	4
Chocolate	4 × 4 oz
Kendal mint cake	4 × 2 oz
Nuts and raisins	4 pkts
Glucose tablets	4 pkts
Coffee + sugar + milk	Enough for one flask

Shopping List

Salt	One small pkt
Sugar	1½ lb
Coffee	8 oz
Cooking oil	1 small bottle
Margarine	4 oz
Oxo	4
Chocolate	12 × 4 oz blocks
Chocolate biscuits	8
Ready Brek	4 oz of raw
Bacon	8 oz
Sausage – pork	8 oz
Baked beans – tinned	8 oz
Braised steak – tinned	1 lb
Potatoes – Smash	Enough to make 1 lb
Carrots – tinned	8 oz
Peas – tinned	1 lb
Rice pudding	24 oz
Bread sliced	One large loaf
Cheese spread	8 oz
Meat spread	8 oz
Nuts and raisins	12 pkts
Fruit pies – single	4
Cans of pop	8
Apples	4
Oranges	4
Cake	One slab cake
Plain biscuits	One pkt
Drinking chocolate	2 oz
Mint cake	4 × 2oz blocks
Glucose tablets	4 pkts
Milk	7 pts (6 pts bought on route)
Eggs	4 (bought on route)
Gravy	1 small pkt
Tea bags	

Now find out the total cost and divide by four to find out the cost of food per person.

LESSON 14: PRODUCING 'COURSES OF ACTION'

Objective

To give a clear understanding of the third stage in the problem-solving process. This third stage is the production of diverse 'courses of action' to deal with the same problem.

Resources

Exercise books

Content

From a selection of problems (various ideas are given in the Teacher Notes) ask the students to 'formulate', identify the major 'elements' and produce as many 'courses of action' as they possibly can for each of them.

Point out to the students, at the end of the lesson, that because many 'courses of action' are possible for each problem, this highlights the importance of the next stage in the problem-solving process which is 'decision-making'. This involves 'evaluating' each 'course of action' and selecting one, or a combination of appropriate ideas.

Assignment

'Formulate' the following problem, identify the major 'elements' and produce as many varied 'courses of action' as possible.

Problem

You have promised to provide a meal for two friends and find out at the last minute that you have run out of potatoes.

Teacher Notes

The first two stages of the problem-solving process should have now developed, in the students, the ability to understand clearly any given problem situation. They should also have generated possible varied directions for 'courses of action' to be constructed, by the consideration of the various strategies available to overcome 'obstacles' and through 'interpretation'.

As I have mentioned earlier, we have a tendency to be satisfied with our first solution, and switch off or produce an answer from stock, if one is available, and then we have great difficulty in finding alternative 'courses of action', even if we want to. Having a system to follow which enables the students to apply their skills to any problem situation, in the knowledge that it will give them a clearer understanding of it, as well as generating possible avenues to pursue, can only be a good thing. Edward de Bono (1973) says, 'The ultimate aim of the thinking lessons is very similar to that of coaching in sport: to make the basic operations of thinking second nature so that they are carried out automatically, smoothly and without fuss or effort.'

Another consideration, mentioned in Lesson 6, is that the actual situation itself can inhibit our ability to think and this problem-solving process helps us to escape from its constraints. Students need to be reminded of the inhibiting factor of one's immediate response to a situation or the terminology used, to help them overcome these components by being aware of them. The problem of having our ability to think creatively restricted by this influence, will also be considered as an important constraining feature in the initial stage of the design process, covered later in this book.

It is also important to remember our natural tendency to reject immediately ideas which appear foolish at first glance (see Lesson 6). All ideas must be considered and fully evaluated before they are dismissed as being unworkable or unacceptable.

Here is a selection of problems for the students to consider:

1. It is essential for you to go from Leeds to Bradford this Sunday but there is a bus workers' strike.
2. There is a ferry workers' strike at Lymington and you need to deliver a lorry load of rowing boats to Yarmouth on the Isle of Wight.
3. Pupils tend to slam the desk lids in your school, creating far too much noise, especially first thing in the morning, and you would like to do something about it.
4. You have lost the key for the lock on your bicycle padlock and chain and you want to go home. The chain is around the back wheel and a metal drainpipe and you need your bicycle that evening to go fishing with your friends at a pond 10 miles away.
5. You need a large circle on a blackboard in your classroom but unfortunately there isn't a large compass in the school.

I have found it suitable to allow the students approximately 10 minutes per problem, then additional time between each one to discuss and share ideas.

Some possible solutions to the above problems are shown overleaf.

1. *Objective*
To go to Bradford on Sunday

Obstacle
Bus workers' strike in Leeds on Sunday

Elements
Leeds, Bradford, bus workers, strike, yourself, reason for going, the bus company, the bus, Sunday

Courses of Action
(a)　Go by train;
(b)　Walk;
(c)　Boat on canal;
(d)　Bicycle;
(e)　Taxi;
(f)　Friend's car;
(g)　Hire a car;
(h)　Own car;
(i)　Aeroplane;

(j) Helicopter;
(k) Horse;
(l) Walk/run;
(m) Roller skates;
(n) Skateboard;
(o) Motorbike;
(p) Scooter;
(q) Use a different bus company;
(r) Girocopter;
(s) Ask someone from Bradford to collect you;
(t) If the strike is in Leeds only, go out of Leeds, to a different area, and catch a bus to Bradford;
(u) Hitch-hike;
(v) Sledge/skis;
(w) Ask police – if important enough;
(x) Make some transport, e.g. cart/go-cart;
(y) Go on Saturday and stay overnight;
(z) Hovercraft;
(aa) Try to settle the strike.

2. *Objective*
To deliver a load of rowing boats to Yarmouth to meet a deadline

Obstacle
Ferry workers' strike at Lymington

Elements
Lymington, Yarmouth, Isle of Wight, ferry workers, ferry, sea, lorry, rowing boats, the firm receiving the boats, strike, ferry company

Courses of Action
(a) Use a different port;
(b) Try to settle the strike;
(c) Take them across by aeroplane;
(d) Hire a different boat to take them across;
(e) Hire a boat to tow them across;
(f) Row them across;
(g) Postpone the delivery date;
(h) Ask someone from the firm at Yarmouth to pick them up;
(i) Use the hovercraft;
(j) Make an arrangement with a firm, making rowing boats, on the Isle of Wight, to deliver some of their boats to Yarmouth, whilst their opposites at Lymington fulfil some orders on the mainland for the Isle of Wight firm.

3. *Objective*
To reduce, especially first thing in the morning, the volume of noise made by pupils slamming desk lids.

Obstacle
School desk lids, when closed quickly, tend to make a noise

Elements
Pupils, yourself, desks, lids, school, noise, morning

Courses of Action
(a) Staff could punish pupils who slam desks;
(b) Purchase new desks without opening lids;
(c) Attach a devise to each desk which only allows the desk lids to close slowly;
(d) Attach padding to the underside of each desk lid;
(e) Fasten down the lids;
(f) Do not use the desks for storing pupils' work;
(g) Wear ear protection;
(h) Do not go into the areas where desks are slammed;
(i) Do not allow pupils to use the desks in the morning;
(j) Go to another school.

4. *Objective*
To go fishing with your friends that evening

Obstacle
Your bicycle is attached by a lock and chain to a metal drainpipe and you have lost the lock key

Elements
Yourself, lock, key, chain, drainpipe, fishing, friends, bicycles, back wheel, pond, 10 miles, home, the location of the bicycle, the location of the home

Courses of Action
(a) Pick the lock;
(b) Leave the bicycle and find another means of transport to the pond;
(c) Break the chain;
(d) Break the lock with a heavy object;
(e) Remove the back wheel and leave it, then purchase or borrow another;
(f) Go home and acquire a spare key;
(g) Remove or break the drainpipe;
(h) Phone the police or fire brigade for help;
(i) Contact a garage;
(j) Ask your friends to go fishing to a pond nearer home.

5. *Objective*
To produce a large circle on a blackboard

Obstacle
No large compass in school

Elements
Circle, blackboard, classroom, compass, school, yourself

Courses of Action
(a) Draw a circle freehand;
(b) Draw around a large circular object;
(c) Cut a circle out of paper and attach it to the blackboard;
(d) Purchase or make a circular blackboard;
(e) Cut a hole in the blackboard;
(f) Use string, chalk and a drawing pin;
(g) Make a compass or a device to draw circles;
(h) Use an overhead projector or slide projector to magnify a small circle;
(i) Draw a small circle and issue special glasses which will magnify it.

Possible Solutions to the Given Assignment

Objective
Provide a meal sometime that day

Obstacle
Run out of potatoes

Elements
Yourself, meal, two friends, last minute, no potatoes, promised, location and surrounding of your house, location and surroundings of your friends' houses.

Courses of Action
(a) Use an alternative to potatoes, for example rice, bread, dumplings, pasta;
(b) Produce a meal which does not require potatoes;
(c) Dig some out of the garden;
(d) Borrow some from a neighbour;
(e) Buy some from a local shop;
(f) Buy some from a local farm;
(g) Take your friends out for a meal near your home;
(h) Take your friends out for a meal near their homes;
(i) Go out and buy a takeaway;
(j) Go out and buy a ready-made, frozen meal and heat it up;
(k) Ask another friend to make a meal for the three of you;
(l) Contact a catering firm who will deliver a ready-made meal to your house.

When 'courses of action' are being considered, to overcome a problem which has been carefully 'formulated', they should be directions which would go part or all of the way to achieving the objective. 'Courses of action' to the above assignment, such as postponing the meal, telling them your cooker has broken down, and something else very important has cropped up, do not even go part of the way. We can only assume from the timing in the problem, that is, 'at the last minute', that you have promised the meal on that particular day. If, however, we could have 'formulated' an objective with a different time element, such as 'To provide a meal at some time for the two friends', we could then consider the additional delaying tactics, mentioned above, as acceptable, additional 'courses of action'.

LESSON 15: THE 'DECISION-MAKING' PROCESS

Objective

To give students a clear understanding of a process which involves the production of lists of criteria (elements). This can be used to make decisions in a constructive way.

Resource

Exercise books
Large selection of vacuum cleaner pamphlets (or any other pamphlets with a reasonable, varied selection of makes and models, e.g. washing machines, videos, fridges) with current prices.

Content

Establish a recognisable process such as the one that follows, which the students can apply to choosing an item, selecting a piece of information or deciding on a course of action.

1. Examine the available items, information or courses of action and prepare a criterion for preference.

2. Decide on a suitable evaluation procedure.

3. Evaluate each of them according to the chosen procedure.

4. Isolate the most suitable item(s), information or course(s) of action.

5. If more than one of the above meet the preferred criteria, additional restrictions, preferences or techniques must be introduced to resolve the situation.

6. Make the decision to carry out the final choice.

Issue a selection of vacuum cleaner pamphlets (or others). These will need to be circulated unless large numbers of them can be obtained.

Using the above process, ask the students to choose which cleaner they would buy. At the end of the exercise conduct a class consensus on the initial list of criteria. The students can then compare it with their own order of preference or priority.

In addition to the above exercise, the students can also use the 'courses of action' which were produced for the last lesson's assignment (meal problem) and produce a criterion for preference to select an appropriate solution.

Assignment

Choose one of the following 'decision-making' situations and apply the above process to help you. Show all the stages in your answer.

1. You have been told that you can have any kind of pet but do not know which one to choose.

2. You live near a volcano which has become active and molten lava is travelling towards your house. You have a maximum of five minutes to pack a medium-sized suitcase. What would you take?

Teacher Notes

This procedure of 'decision-making' aids the process of choosing between all the alternatives by giving one a technique by which evaluation can take place. This ensures that of the choices available the final outcome meets, as nearly as possible, the initial criteria. It also helps one to avoid making decisions which are influenced by emotion, prejudices or stereotypes.

Using the information given on the pamphlets ask the students to draw up a list of criteria (elements) that will help them to see everything that new vacuum cleaners have on offer, for example:

(a) Length of guarantee;
(b) Type of external container;
(c) The cost of the machine;
(d) Method of holding and disposing of dust;
(e) The capacity of the dust container;
(f) The colours that are available;
(g) The weight of the machine;
(h) The reputation of the cleaner or company;
(i) Ease of maintenance;
(j) Availability of spares;
(k) The cost of spares;
(l) Length of flex;
(m) Storage of flex;
(n) The power of the motor;
(o) The type of model, e.g. upright or cylinder;
(p) Availability of attachments;
(q) The variety of attachments;
(r) Up-to-dateness of technology;
(s) The overall size of the cleaner;
(t) The storage of the machine;
(u) The noise level of the working machine;
(v) Free electric plug issued with the machine;
(w) Air freshener attachment;
(x) The appearance and shape of the model;
(y) The country of origin;
(z) The manoeuvrability of the cleaner when in use;
(aa) The size of the cleaner's nozzle;
(bb) The type of cleaning action (suction, brush, rotary brush);
(cc) Variable speeds available;
(dd) Light on the front.

This should be followed by a class discussion to share ideas and will enable all the students to have as many criteria as possible for consideration.

Now apply the 'decision-making' process described in the lesson content.

1. Preparation of a criterion for preference, e.g. 'The cleaner that I would prefer must be an upright model with a total cost of less than £150.' In my case there are no other definite criteria that I would insist upon, but others may have far more or, alternatively, no particular restrictions at all.

2. A suitable procedure to evaluate the remaining criteria could be to give each of them a score or, alternatively, to produce a new list in your order of importance or preference, then in descending order give each a score.

For example, since there are thirty criteria, the first would receive thirty points and the last only one point. Each element would also have to be given additional lower scores depending upon the number of variations it contains, e.g. the type of external container. It could be plastic, metal or cloth, and you may give a much lower score for metal or plastic if cloth was your preference.

3. All the criteria would be applied to individual vacuum cleaners and a total for each model would be produced.

4. The vacuum cleaner or cleaners with the highest scores are then isolated from the rest.

5. If more than one cleaner remains, the criteria must once again be considered, one at a time in descending order, until one of the vacuums ends up with a higher score. It may end up with the choice of colour or the noise level being the deciding factor.

If a company who manufactured vacuum cleaners wanted to find out what the majority of the public were looking for when buying a new cleaner, they would have a team of market researchers conduct a consensus on the general public. I have found it quite an interesting exercise to use the students' lists of criteria, which they have arranged in order of preference, to produce a class consensus so that the students can compare their own list with the amalgamated one.

I think that I would be quite safe in saying that at some time we have all made a wrong or poor decision. As mentioned earlier in Lesson 11 it is very useful to be aware how easily our initial perception of the problem can be influenced by our emotions and prejudices. Therefore, it is worth considering some possible causes of careless decision-making in the hope that this knowledge will help us to avoid them.

Some of these causes could be:

1. Following the wrong objective.
2. Having an unclear objective.
3. Not having all the available information.
4. A lack of concern about the outcome.
5. Wanting to take the easy way out.
6. Having personal prejudices and reacting to emotions.
7. Trying to relate it to similar past experiences and assuming that it will be the same outcome.
8. Being impatient and acting impulsively.
9. Relying on someone else's ability to make the decision for you.

> 'In all this discussion of decision-making it is easy to overlook the fact that nobody can tell another person exactly how he should make a decision. The decision maker has to take himself into account. Only he knows the truth about the personal values to be put into the equation. In other words, in making any practical decision there may be an ethical or moral element which is outside the scope of our methodical approach.'
>
> *Professor K. F. Jackson* (1983)

TEST 1: THE PROBLEM-SOLVING PROCESS I

1¼ hours allowed

Answer all the following questions.

1. Make a list of all the major elements in the following:
   (d) Sports bag,
   (b) Cabinet maker's screwdriver,
   (c) I am very tired, but I cannot go to bed for another two hours until I have finished my work.

2. State the main obstacle in the following problems:
   (a) I would like to go on holiday but I have only £1 left.
   (b) It is snowing outside and I would like to play football.
   (c) We were going to fly my kite but we could not find it and the last time we used it, the kite was damaged beyond repair.

3. State the objective in the following problems:
   (a) I am very thirsty; the electric kettle has broken down; I have run out of milk, tea bags and coffee and the water has been turned off.
   (b) I have promised to visit my sister for the weekend. Unfortunately someone has dumped a very large load of sand in front of my car which is still parked in my drive. The sand belongs to my neighbour. There is such a large amount of sand that it would take one person at least half a day to move it. The time is 9 am on Saturday.
   (c) I work late every evening which means that I do not arrive home until 7 pm. I would like to see my little girl before she goes to sleep, but unfortunately she is put into bed at 6 pm.

4. If the formula for a problem is P = O + O, make the following into problems:
   (a) I want to catch the 8 am bus.
   (b) I want to watch 'Top of the Pops' on T.V.
   (c) My new dress is torn.
   (d) My shoes are dirty.

5. Examine the picture overleaf and then answer the following:
   (a) Formulate the problem.
   (b) Make a list of major elements.
   (c) Produce as many different courses of action to deal with the situation as you can. (The solutions can be either temporary or permanent.)
   (d) Evaluate each of your solutions and make a decision as to which of them, in your opinion, is the appropriate action to implement. Give reasons for your choice.

Sketches must be used where necessary.

Use this picture with Question 5 in Test 1

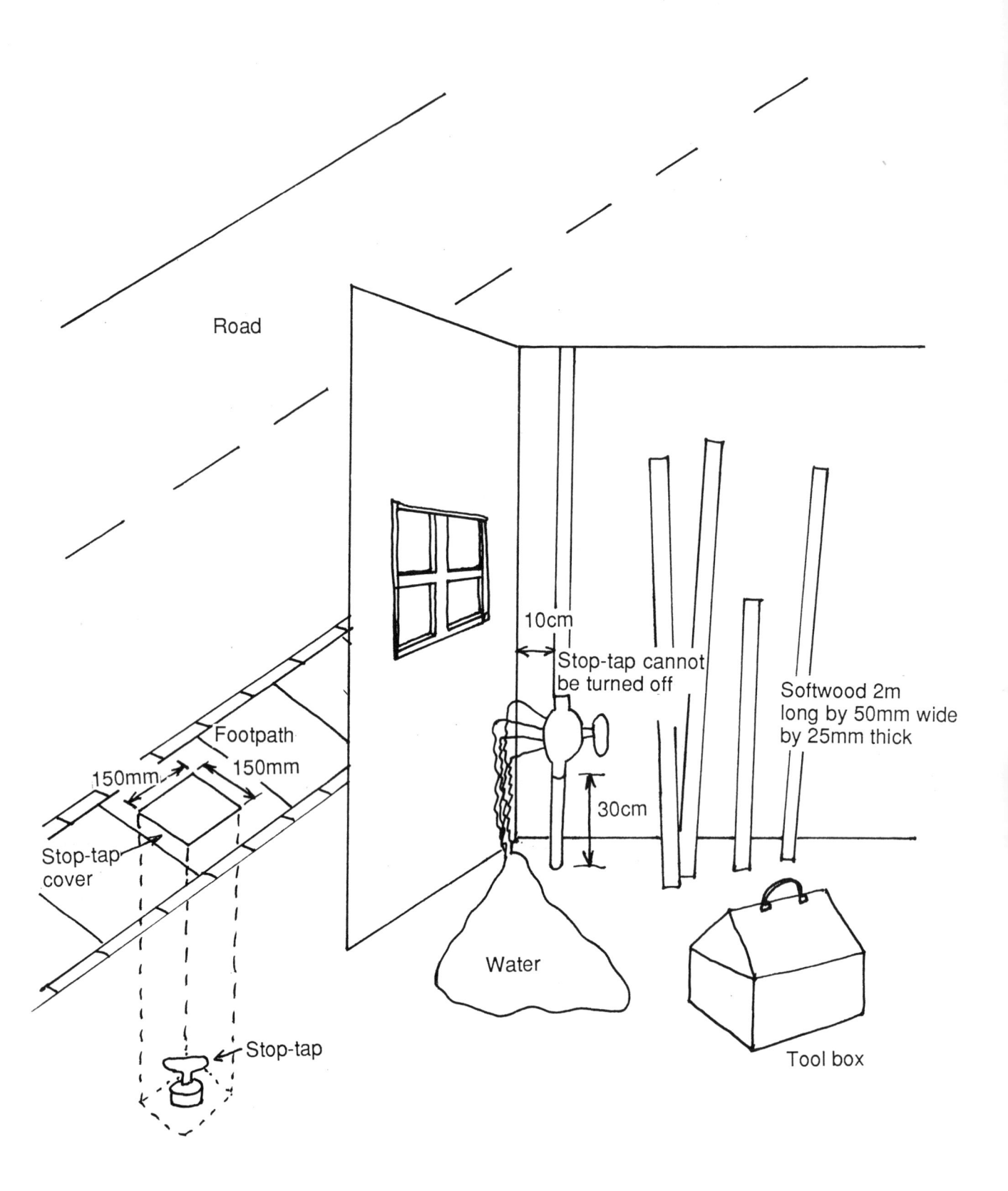

The picture shows a burst, internal stop-top in your own house, and because it is the actual stop-tap that has fractured, the flow of water cannot be turned off at this point.

It is a bad leak and the water is gushing out with force against the side wall which is only 10 cm away.

Outside, set into the footpath, is a metal plate measuring 15 cm × 15 cm which covers up another stop-tap which is 1 m deep and well out of reach of the hand. You do not have any plumbing equipment, but as well as having the normal items found in a household, you also have the items shown in the picture. The tool box contains the typical tools one would expect to find in a normal household.

The time is 12 midnight and you must do something about the situation.

Test 1 Marking Scheme

This contains answers and specimen answers.

Marks

1a.	Container, method of transporting (handle) fastenings, fitments	4
1b.	Handle, shaft, blade	3
1c.	Yourself, the work, place of work, bed, 2 hrs, time, tired, home, journey home, surroundings of the place of work	6
2a.	Only £1	2
2b.	Snow	2
2c.	Kite beyond repair	4
3a.	To quench thirst	4
3b.	To visit sister	4
3c.	To see little girl before she goes to sleep	4
4a	Obstacle needed, e.g. '. . . but I cannot find any money.'	4
4b.	Obstacle needed, e.g. '. . . but the set has broken down.'	4
4c.	Objective needed, e.g. 'I was going to a party tonight.'	4
4d.	Objective needed, e.g. 'I want to walk across the carpet.'	4
		50

5. *Objective:* to prevent the water damaging the property or contents.   4

   Obstacle: the internal stop-tap has burst.   4

   Elements: pipe, water, stop-tap (inside), stop-tap (outside), road, path, stop-tap cover, gap between path and house, tool box, tools, wood, household contents, house (including walls, windows, floors etc.).   8

   Courses of action: these could include:
   (a) Apply tape or binding.
   (b) Call a 24-hour plumber.

(c) Make a device to turn off the outside stop-tap.
(d) Divert the flow of water, e.g. divert the water into a container and keep emptying with a smaller vessel, syphon out of container using a hosepipe through the window, use guttering to channel the water outside.
(e) Cut pipe and place a hosepipe over it and then divert it outside through the window.
(f) Cut the pipe and bend it over.
(g) Squash the pipe below the leak with pliers or a hammer.
(h) Cut pipe then bung it up with a wooden plug.
(i) Turn all the other taps on in the house to try and reduce the pressure of water through the split or hole. Then try and force something into the gap in the stop-tap to block the flow of water.
(j) Lift some floorboards so that the water drains away.
(k) Knock a hole in the wall so that it gushes straight outside.
(l) Dig down in the soft earth outside the wall and break the pipe to prevent water reaching the burst. 20

Evaluation of each course of action: e.g. knocking a hole in the wall would probably cause more damage than the water and some of the other possibilities appear less drastic, therefore it is not the best solution. 10

Final decision: selection of an appropriate solution or combination of solutions. 4
                                                                                    ——
                                                                                    50

TEST 2: THE PROBLEM-SOLVING PROCESS II

1¼ hours allowed

Answer all the following questions.

1. Make a list of all the major elements in the following:
   (a) Saucepan
   (b) Suitcase
   (c) I am very hungry but I will not arrive home for tea for another two hours.

2. State the main objective in each of the following problems:
   (a) I would like to sit down but the rocking chair will not bear my weight because the screws have been lost out of one of the rockers.
   (b) My front window does not have a curtain rail and I do not want people to look into the room.
   (c) The electric fire is broken and I am very cold.

3. State the main obstacle in each of the following problems:
   (a) I would like to go to the pictures but my friend has phoned to say that he cannot go and I have also misplaced my money.
   (b) I was going to visit a friend but I have lost his address and my car has broken down.

4. A problem is created when you have an objective plus an obstacle. Make the following into problems by adding a few extra words of your own choice.
   (a) I would like to drive a train.
   (b) The battery in my torch is flat.
   (c) The television plug is missing.
   (d) The fridge is empty.
   (e) We were going to the gymnasium.

5. Examine the picture overleaf and then answer the following:
   (a) Formulate the problem.
   (b) Make a list of the major elements.
   (c) Produce as many different courses of action to deal with the situation as you can. (The solutions can be either temporary or permanent.)
   (d) Evaluate each of your solutions and make a decision as to which of them, in your opinion, is the appropriate action to implement. Give reasons for your choice.

   Sketches must be used where necessary.

   The picture shows a tropical fish tank measuring 2 m × 600 mm × 600 mm, containing 340 litres of water at a temperature of 26°C, the temperature needed to keep the 10 flesh-eating piranha fish alive.

Use this picture with Question 5 in Test 2

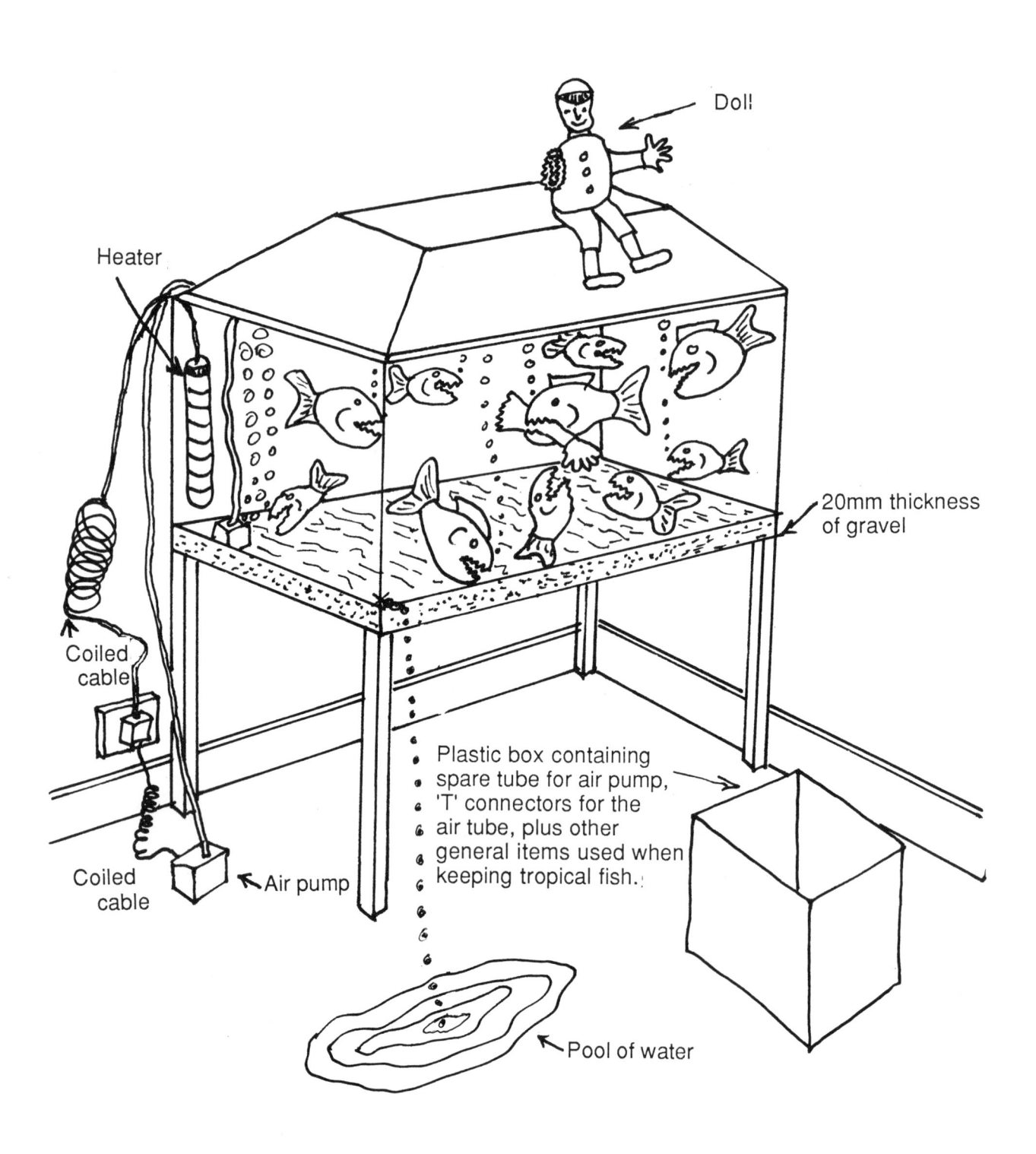

- Doll
- Heater
- Coiled cable
- Coiled cable
- Air pump
- 20mm thickness of gravel
- Plastic box containing spare tube for air pump, 'T' connectors for the air tube, plus other general items used when keeping tropical fish.
- Pool of water

The all-glass tank has sprung a leak in the silicone jointing compound, 25 mm from the bottom left hand side of the tank and water is running onto the carpet on the living room floor.

The full tank of water is far too heavy to lift, even by two strong adults.

The sound of water running from the tank woke you up at 1 am on Saturday morning and you have to do something about the situation.

Test 2 Marking Scheme

This contains answers and specimen answers.

		Marks
1a.	Handle, container, lid, fastenings and fitments	4
1b.	Method of carrying, container, fastenings (hinges, locks etc.) fitments	4
1c.	Hunger, myself, home, time, the place where you are, 2 hours, tea-time, method of travelling home, the thing that is preventing you from going home.	9
2a.	To sit down	4
2b.	Privacy	4
2c.	To keep warm	4
3a.	No money	3
3b.	Lost address	3
4a.	Obstacle needed, e.g. '. . . but I am not old enough.'	3
4b.	Objective needed, e.g. '. . . and I wanted to use the torch to help me to see in the loft.'	3
4c.	Objective needed, e.g. 'and I wanted to watch a programme.'	3
4d.	Objective needed, e.g. 'and I wanted some ice cubes to cool down my drink.'	3
4e.	Obstacle needed, e.g. '. . . but I have lost my shorts.'	3
		50

5. *Objective:* to prevent the fish from dying and prevent any further damage to the carpet or floor.   4

Obstacle: a small area of silicone sealer is no longer adhering to the glass on the lower part of the joint and is allowing a small stream of water to escape.   4

Elements: the fish, water, tank, air pump, plastic box, heater, coiled cable, spare tube, 'T' connector, additional contents in box, doll, carpet, tank support, tank hood, gravel, leak, silicone glue, time, floor, house contents, yourself.   8

Courses of action: this could include:
(a) Apply self-adhesive tape or other 'sticky' substance, e.g. chewing gum, silglass etc., inside or outside the tank.
(b) Transfer the fish, water and heater into another container, e.g. plastic box, spare tank, bath, sink.

- (c) Contact a friend who has a spare tank.
- (d) Reduce the volume of water in the tank and tilt it to raise the leak above the water level. Remove gravel to make more space for fish.
- (e) Devise some method of using the air pump to transfer the water back into the tank as it runs out.
- (f) Stay up all night with a bucket recycling it back into the tank.
- (g) Seal around the top of the tank after removing the air pump.
- (h) Place a bin liner inside the tank and transfer the fish, water and heater into it.   20

Evaluation of each course of action.   10

Final decision: selection of an appropriate solution or combination of solutions.   4

    50

Part III

SUMMARY

This section is devoted to the process of designing. The format I have chosen is shown overleaf.

Each stage has been developed and is followed by a complete worked example of a project which starts from a problem situation and develops into a design brief.

Finally there is a bank of problem and design situations for the students who have difficulty in finding their own problems or situations.

HOW TO DESIGN SOMETHING

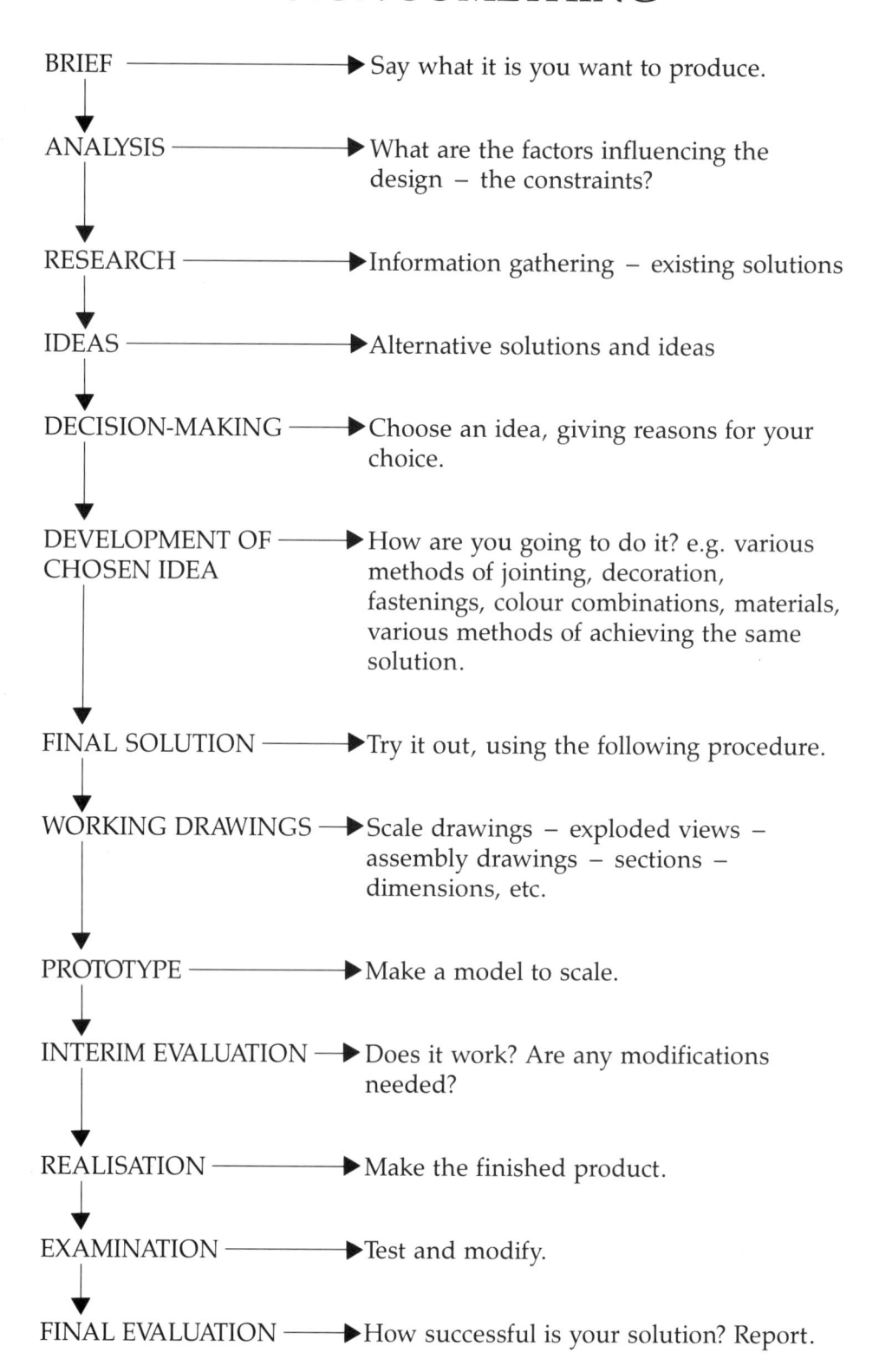

BRIEF ⟶ Say what it is you want to produce.

ANALYSIS ⟶ What are the factors influencing the design – the constraints?

RESEARCH ⟶ Information gathering – existing solutions

IDEAS ⟶ Alternative solutions and ideas

DECISION-MAKING ⟶ Choose an idea, giving reasons for your choice.

DEVELOPMENT OF CHOSEN IDEA ⟶ How are you going to do it? e.g. various methods of jointing, decoration, fastenings, colour combinations, materials, various methods of achieving the same solution.

FINAL SOLUTION ⟶ Try it out, using the following procedure.

WORKING DRAWINGS ⟶ Scale drawings – exploded views – assembly drawings – sections – dimensions, etc.

PROTOTYPE ⟶ Make a model to scale.

INTERIM EVALUATION ⟶ Does it work? Are any modifications needed?

REALISATION ⟶ Make the finished product.

EXAMINATION ⟶ Test and modify.

FINAL EVALUATION ⟶ How successful is your solution? Report.

NOTES ON THE DESIGN PROCESS

The Brief

When writing a brief from which to work it is essential that a clear statement of what you wish to achieve is produced in an unrestrictive form. For example, if a brief states 'design an egg cup', it immediately has the effect of conjuring up a fixed shape in your mind and makes further progress difficult. If the function is clearly stated in terms of what you wish to achieve, e.g. 'design something which could support a boiled egg whilst you eat it', this gives the imagination much more freedom to develop ideas.

'Design an egg cup' is also unsuitable because 'an egg cup' is not the description of a design problem but the description of a solution to a problem.

At this stage it should be noted that during the problem-solving process an exact 'formulation' can often generate new ideas; however, the reverse can be said about exact definitions when producing a design brief.

The influence of the brief upon our ability to think creatively is also mentioned in the 'Problem-Solving Module' produced by the 'Schools Council Modular Courses in Technology' group (1982). They say:

> 'If we had said design a corkscrew in the previous section, this would have pre-empted any other method. Similarly, if you were asked to design a pair of nutcrackers, the use of the words "pair of nutcrackers" tends to suggest there is only one way to crack a nut . . . The development of correction fluid, which allows a typist to cover up her mistake with a quick-drying white liquid that can be typed on again almost instantaneously, was feasible several years before it occurred. The delay was probably because the words "rub out" led developers away from thinking in terms of "cover up".'

In the problem-solving module above it also suggests that 'limitations' should be considered before constructing a brief and producing specifications. There are occasions, such as designing hardware for a customer, when strict limitations and specifications are put on the brief before it is constructed. As I have mentioned, this could result in the production of a very restrictive brief which could have detrimental effects on the ability of the mind to be creative.

Using the minimum number of constraints at the start does not mean that the end product will not meet the final requirements. This is because, during analysis, the second stage in the design process, all the limitations and specifications will be considered before the 'development of ideas' and the production of a 'final decision'.

Analysis

This stage is to do with the initial exploration of the brief, including the consideration of the inherent specifications, and is not intended to produce any immediate solutions.

The 'analysis' of the initial statement; that is a complete breakdown of the problem into its 'elements', could include such things as identifying important functions, further information needed and how one proposes to obtain it, including thoughts about:

(a) Which form can it take?
(b) Suitable colours and methods of application?
(c) Are there any size limitations?
(d) Are there any weight limitations?
(e) How and where can the item be stored?
(f) Are there any cost limitations?
(g) Which safety precautions are necessary?
(h) Could it be easily cleaned?
(i) Which textures are available or suitable?
(j) How could the strength and durability be increased?
(k) How could the item be made more aesthetically pleasing?
(l) Does the item need to be concealed?
(m) How could the item be concealed?
(n) Which materials are available?
(o) Which processes can be performed on the materials?
(p) How can the material be joined together?
(q) Which methods could be used to create interest?
(r) How easily could it be manufactured?
(s) Could it be combined or used with something else?
(t) Which areas are available for consideration?
(u) How could it be made easy to understand?
(v) Does it need to be adaptable?
(w) How could it be made more adaptable?
(x) Who will assemble the finished product?
(y) Will instructions be required if the item is self-assembly?
(z) Which type of packaging would be suitable?
(aa) Does the item require packaging?
(bb) Which areas of the market could be considered?
(cc) What is already available on the market?

As well as considering some of the above points, it is now important to remember some of the lessons in the earlier stages of this book.

In Lesson 1 (page 6) we considered the availability of ready-made patterns and ideas which could be taken from our natural surroundings, or even imagining ourselves with all nature's skills at our disposal.

Lesson 6 (page 36) covered alternative uses for everyday items. This can be a very useful technique in generating new or alternative ideas. It involves taking an existing solution or idea and applying various processes such as the ones shown below.

1. Re-arranging its components,
2. Altering its shape,

3. Increasing or reducing its size,
4. Combining it with something else,
5. Changing its position or direction,
6. Finding alternative uses.

Lesson 12 (page 73) also generates a very useful process in helping creativity to flourish. This involves writing down the elements from an existing solution but in such a way as not to restrict the thinking process, in the same way that care should be given to the wording of the brief.

Here is an example of how the elements of one of the items from Lesson 12 could be written down in order to encourage creativity.

Torch – elements

1. (bulb) light source,
2. (battery) power source,
3. (lens) protection and concentration of light source,
4. (container) container for light and power source,
5. (switch) method of releasing and extinguishing light source,
6. fastenings and fitments,
7. (reflector) redirecting light source.

Research

Each of the elements appropriate to the problem should now be applied and considered and further information gathered about each area of analysis.

Whenever I can, I prefer to leave the implementation of the precise specification and limitations on the design as late as possible, because I find that they can have an inhibiting factor on the creative process.

The gathering of information including simple facts and figures and specific details can be obtained from personal experience, observation, discussion, listening and from written material.

Pictures cut from magazines should be used with discretion because they can often give one a set of stereotyped ideas which would end up with the solution being merely an exercise in copying.

Ideas and Alternative Solutions

Information gained from the analysis and research should have stimulated the imagination into identifying several different approaches which could be considered for development. It is also worth considering some of the techniques mentioned earlier in this book.

One of the first things that must be considered is to remind ourselves of the inhibiting factors. The first of these is the actual wording of the brief that may have been issued to us. Second, the consideration of the limitations and specifications helps to prevent creative thinking and finally, as mentioned in Lesson 1, our tendency to reject, or not even consider ideas which may at first glance appear silly or impossible. Fear of criticism is strongly connected with this final factor.

The technique I used in Lesson 7 (page 41) for generating ideas (the inverted frying pan) at first glance appears silly, and traditionalists may reject its potential as a useful exercise without giving the process a fair trial. Taking a ready-made solution can influence and inhibit the creative process but experimentation with such a product can also be useful. Such solutions can also be improved by building new ideas onto them.

The strategies we considered in Lesson 11 (page 70) which helped to overcome obstacles are once again worth considering at this stage, along with the technique we used in Lesson 6 (page 36). This was concerned with finding alternative uses for everyday objects. It would involve considering items which have no connection with the area of the design.

Isolating the elements from a ready-made solution and writing them down in the same way as shown in the analysis section can generate alternative ideas. Applying the six processes, also mentioned in the same stage, to each of the elements can also generate new or different ideas. The same can be said if they are applied to a complete ready-made solution.

If several other people are available, it is worth considering using the technique of brainstorming. Once again it is important to record all the ideas generated and not reject any 'unsuitable' suggestions until they have been fully explored. Some spontaneous suggestions may appear outlandish at first glance but on closer examination may generate some useful avenues to follow. When brainstorming it is also worth pointing out at the start that as well as producing totally different ideas, it is also necessary to build onto ideas already generated by the group.

Combining different ideas can also be useful in the generation of ideas or developing creativity.

> 'Things which have existed separately are put together to produce something that has a value greater than the sum of its parts.
>
> The process is a relatively easy one to use because there is something to work upon – in contrast to trying to pull an idea out of the air.
>
> For instance, a Victorian invention sought to combine a mouse trap and a cheese grater – without great advantage to either. On the other hand the combination of a tiny torch and a key ring had definite advantages when one was trying to find a key hole in the dark.'
>
> Edward de Bono (1975)

The last technique I am going to mention in this stage is the use of 'lateral thinking'. Whereas divergent thinking develops a multiplicity of alternatives, the end product of lateral thinking is an insight to the situation.

Any ideas which are generated by the above processes should take the form of annotated sketches so that the person's thoughts are clearly recorded in the sequence they occur. The accompanying notes are very important because they provide the opportunity for self-comment, e.g. 'This looks promising because . . .', 'this will not work because . . .'.

Having considered each of the different approaches, the most promising should then be identified for further development, giving reasons for the choice.

Development of the Chosen Idea

Before selecting the final idea to develop, it is necessary to check that your choice meets, as near as possible, with the original brief and the limitations and specifications which have been imposed upon it. This will include such considerations as cost limitations, legal requirements and time limitations.

Ideas about the most promising approach are developed and expressed in the form of more annotated sketchwork. Various methods of jointing the item, as well as safety, alternative fastenings, colour combinations, decorations, materials and alternative ways of achieving the same solution are considered and then finalised. Tests may be conducted and results recorded. Production techniques are worked out and aesthetic factors considered. Models can also be useful at this stage to help clarify and explain some problems. These can be photographed or dismantled to display in the final folio.

This stage concludes with a firm proposal for a developed solution to the problem.

Working Drawing

This usually means any type of drawing that contains enough information, appropriately presented, to enable a competent person to realise the design without any further information, exactly as the designer intended.

This section could include scale drawings, exploded views, assembly drawings, isometric or pictorial sketches, sections and dimensions.

Interim Evaluation

It is now often advisable to make a scale model to find out if it works or looks acceptable, and if any modifications are required.

Realisation

The finished product can now be made, further tests applied, and, if needed, modifications carried out.

Final Evaluation

A final report on the success of the finished solution should now be presented. The basic question which should be considered is 'does it work?'. This is followed by checking whether the solution meets all the requirements of the brief and limitations which may have been imposed. Finally, if you had to tackle this same situation are there any modifications you could make to further improve the final design?

Other questions which could be considered in this final evaluation are:

1. the efficiency of the product,
2. its aesthetic appearance,
3. the running costs,

4. any limitations,
5. the maintenance,
6. the ease of repair,
7. its effects on the environment,
8. any additional uses,
9. its safety both in and out of use.

> 'Designing should not be confused with Art, with Science or with Mathematics. It is a hybrid activity which depends, for its successful execution, upon a proper blending of all three and is most unlikely to succeed if it is exclusively identified with any one.'
>
> *J. Christopher Jones (1970)*

A WORKED EXAMPLE: THE EGG-SUPPORT PROBLEM

The following project demonstrates the whole problem-solving and design process. Although the chosen situation may be seen as rather unrealistic, it is only meant to demonstrate the various techniques mentioned earlier in this book and to show the importance of examination and exploration of a situation before one assumes that there is a need to design something.

I once asked a group of my students to design a play area for a pet white mouse. They had already tackled the problem-solving section from this book so they decided to ask me what was the objective in producing such a play area. I then made the mistake of telling the students that the mouse was unhappy in its little cage (no, I cannot really tell whether a mouse is unhappy). This had the immediate effect of making the group start to use the skills that they had developed. They pointed out to me that there was no need to design a play area, and they gave me several alternative courses of action which could be taken. These included putting a mouse of the opposite sex into the cage with it, providing it with a friend of the same sex, releasing the mouse, buying a bigger cage and the novel suggestion of telling me that the mouse might be unhappy about the colour of its coat and we could try dyeing it black or brown. My objective was really to familiarise the students with the design process and give them a little light relief from the theory work by tackling a practical project. At least their reply meant that some of the students had learnt something from my earlier lessons.

The Egg-support Problem

111

Summary of the Egg-support Problem

You have moved into an isolated house and your furniture and belongings have not yet arrived.

A local farmer called and gave you one of his hens' eggs to sample.

You are very hungry and would like to eat the egg, preferably whilst it is hot and the yoke is still soft. Unfortunately, you have only some scissors, a piece of card, a spoon and the facilities to boil the egg. (The facilities are a gas stove, a pan and a supply of water.)

Objective

To try to stop yourself feeling hungry, preferably by having something to eat.

Obstacle

The egg which is available would probably need some kind of support if it was to be eaten whilst it was hot and the yoke was still soft.

Interpretation

Elements

1. Egg,
2. Yourself,
3. House,
4. Contents,
5. Room, floor, walls, ceiling,
6. Surroundings outside the house,
7. Clothing,
8. Furniture,
9. Farmer,
10. Spoon,
11. Card,
12. Gas cooker,
13. Water,
14. Pan,
15. Scissors,
16. Hungry,
17. Isolation,
18. Eat.

Analysis

1. How many different ways could the egg be cooked?
   Would the yoke solidify if the egg cooled down?
   Do you want to eat the egg when it is cold?
2. Would the egg be too hot to hold in the hand?
   Do you want to change your mind about the temperature and condition of the egg when you eat it?

3. Is there anything lying around the house which could help you to support the egg?
   Is there anything else to eat in the house?

4. Is there a telephone in the house?

5. Are there any articles or fitments in the room which could help to support an egg?
   Are there any knot-holes in the floor?
   Is there anything which could be used to make a hole in the floor?
   Are there any working surfaces or window ledges in the house?
   Could the light fitment or part of it be used to help support an egg?
   Could any part of a door be used to act as an egg support?

6. Is there anything outside the house which could be eaten?
   Do you have any transport?
   Are you close to a bus route? If so, how often do they run?
   Are there any other houses in the area?
   What is growing in the fields around your house?
   Is there anything lying around outside which could be used to support an egg?
   Could you make some kind of egg support from natural objects which can be found outside the house?
   Are any vehicles passing near your house?
   Is there a river or stream nearby containing fish?
   Are there any rabbits or game birds near your house?

7. Could your clothing be used to help support the egg?

8. Has the previous owner left any furniture which may help you support the egg?

9. Is the farmer still in the area?
   How far away does he live?
   Does he have any cows?
   Are there any near your house?

10. Could the spoon be easily bent?
    Would you need the spoon to eat the egg?

11. Could something be made out of card to support the egg?

12. Are there any parts on the gas cooker which could support an egg?

13. Could the water be used to clean a surface somewhere from which to eat the egg?
    How could the egg be cooked in the water?

14. Could the pan be used to support the egg in some way?
    Does the egg have to remain inside the shell whilst it is being cooked or eaten?

15. Could the scissors be used to support the egg?
    Could the scissors be used in conjunction with something else to make an egg support?

16. Is there anything else you can do to prevent you feeling hungry?
    Could you take your mind off feeling hungry by doing some work on or around the house?
    What time is the furniture going to arrive?

17. Is there anyone else going to live with you?
    How far away are the nearest shops?
    Do any mobile shops visit the area?
    Are there any public telephones in the area?

18. When was the last time you had something to eat?
    Could you eat the egg without cooking it?
    Would drinking a lot of water make you feel less hungry?

Research

The above analysis needs to be fully researched to give one a complete picture of the situation. This will enable a full evaluation to be made of each of the courses of action which will be generated by the earlier stages of the problem-solving process.

Courses of Action

Consider all the strategies for overcoming obstacles as well as all the analysis and research.

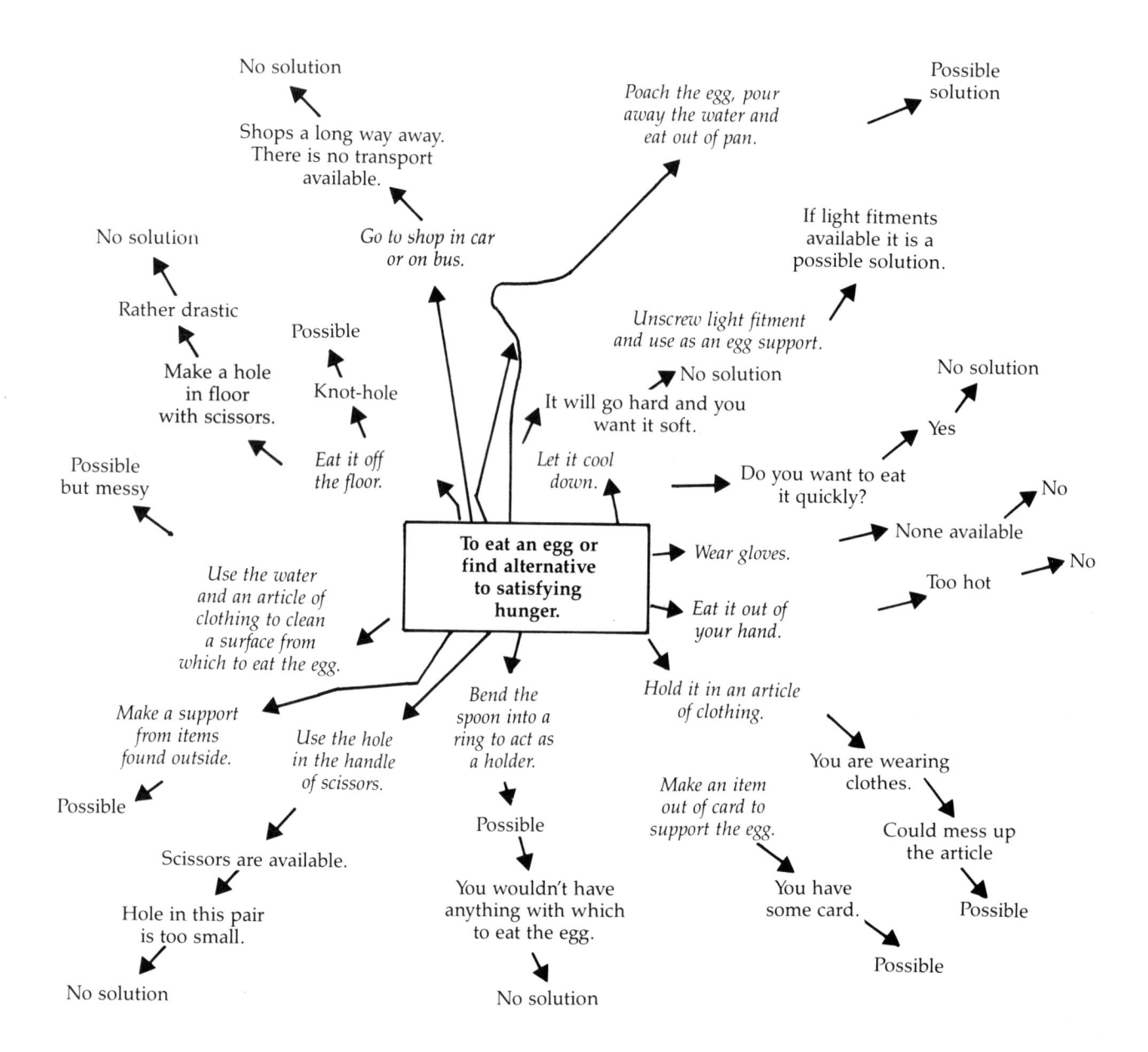

Diagram: Central box "To eat an egg or find alternative to satisfying hunger." with branches:

- Shops a long way away. There is no transport available. → No solution
- Go to shop in car or on bus. → Possible
- Poach the egg, pour away the water and eat out of pan. → Possible solution
- Unscrew light fitment and use as an egg support. → If light fitments available it is a possible solution.
- Make a hole in floor with scissors. → Rather drastic → No solution
- Knot-hole → Possible
- Eat it off the floor. → Possible but messy
- Let it cool down. → It will go hard and you want it soft. → No solution
- Do you want to eat it quickly? → Yes → No solution; → No → None available
- Wear gloves. → None available
- Eat it out of your hand. → Too hot → No
- Use the water and an article of clothing to clean a surface from which to eat the egg.
- Make a support from items found outside. → Possible
- Use the hole in the handle of scissors. → Scissors are available. → Hole in this pair is too small. → No solution
- Bend the spoon into a ring to act as a holder. → Possible → You wouldn't have anything with which to eat the egg. → No solution
- Hold it in an article of clothing. → You are wearing clothes. → Could mess up the article → Possible
- Make an item out of card to support the egg. → You have some card. → Possible

Decision-making

Using the light fitment shade attachment would be a quick alternative to an egg cup, but we do not know if there is definitely one available. Poaching the egg in the water in the pan would also be a very good solution; however, let us imagine that you do not like poached eggs and you want it boiled. This means that it is probably reasonable to make some kind of support out of card to hold the hot egg whilst you eat it. In fact, the time and concentration needed to design an egg support out of card may be an acceptable solution in itself to help you forget about feeling hungry until your belongings arrive.

The Brief

Design and produce a card support for an egg?

Analysis

1. What materials are available?
2. How much card is available?
3. How strong is the card?
4. How could the strength of the card be increased?
5. Could the card be used in conjunction with some of the other items which may be available?
6. Which properties does card possess?
7. How could one fasten together the card?
8. What size does the support need to be?
9. How many eggs do you need to support?
10. Which shapes will support an egg?
11. Does the support need to be free-standing?
12. Will you need to use the egg support again?

Research

1. It is raining very heavily outside and you do not want to go looking for additional materials. This means that card and your clothing are the only materials which are available.
2. There is one piece of card available, 60 cm long by 60 cm wide.
3. The card is fairly thin: approximately 200 microns thick.
4. The strength of the card could be increased by corrugating, rolling, laminating, folding, weaving and interlocking to form cellular structures and using strips of card on their edges.
5. It could be used in conjunction with the clothing, pan, spoon, gas cooker, water.
6. Card can be cut, folded, bent, rolled, embossed, laminated, woven, reconstituted, twisted and shaped.
7. There is no glue, sellotape or any other type of adhesive available; neither are there any materials available which could be used to make your own adhesive. There are no paper clips, hair clips, staples, paper fasteners, pins, needles or any pieces of wire which could be used to attach together the card. It may be possible to make a series of holes in the card with the point of the scissors and use shoe laces, cotton

removed from items of clothing or even cutting or tearing strips from the clothing, to connect the card. Various other techniques such as making slits and tabs, weaving, interlocking etc. can be seen in sketch form in Lesson 8 Teacher Notes (page 45).

8. The size of the egg needs to be measured in some way and the points of contact of the support need to be slightly smaller than the maximum outside circumference of the egg.

9. Only one egg needs to be supported.

10. Because a typical egg support is round on the outside, we must not be influenced into thinking that a circular cup shape is the only alternative available. As well as triangles, squares, pentagons, hexagons and various other shapes of hole which would support an egg, it could also be supported by having different points of contact on the egg. These could be arranged haphazardly or in a vertical plane as opposed to the horizontal one produced by the use of various shaped holes.

11. The support could be free-standing, hand-held or made to be supported by some other item; for example, the pan or the metal framework on top of the gas rings which is used to support the pan.

12. It is very unlikely that the egg support will be used again in the future.

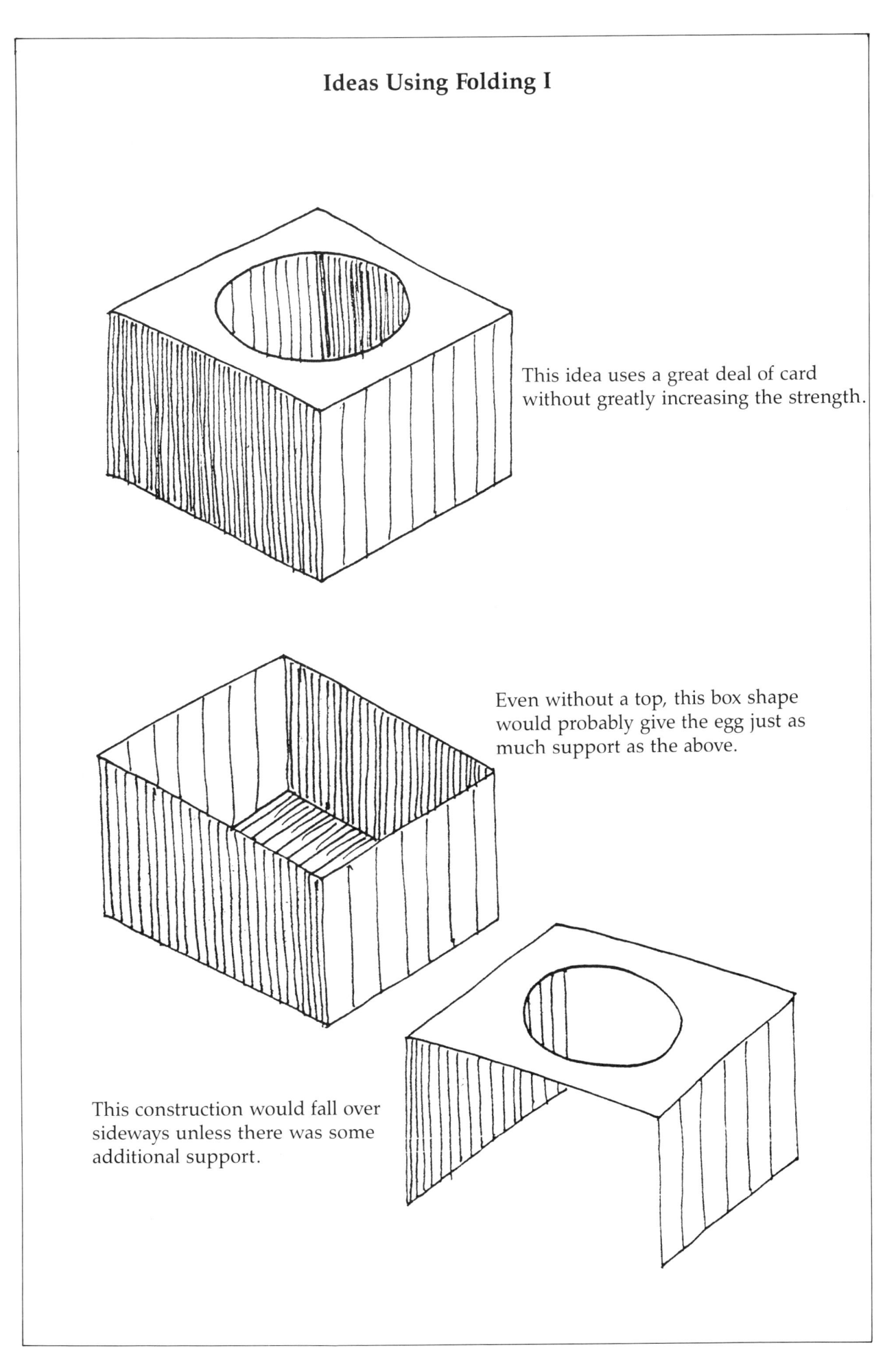

Ideas Using Folding I

This idea uses a great deal of card without greatly increasing the strength.

Even without a top, this box shape would probably give the egg just as much support as the above.

This construction would fall over sideways unless there was some additional support.

Ideas Using Folding II

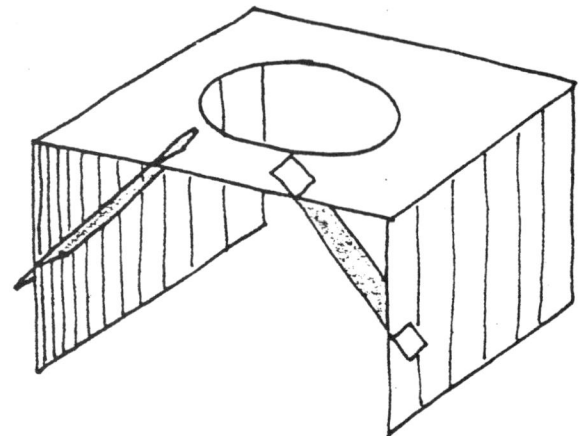

This design still appears rather weak, but the additional supports have slightly increased the strength.

This is very similar to the first idea on the previous page and does not give any additional strength for the increased amount of card.

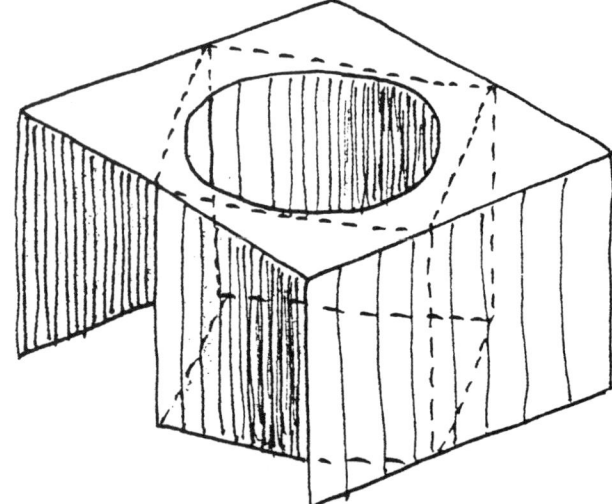

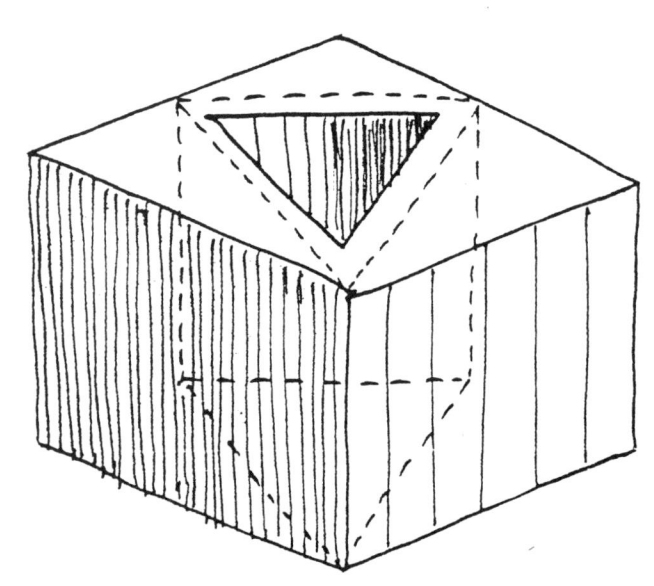

The hole in the top does not have to be round and the additional triangular support under the surface appears to give the outside support additional strength.

Ideas Using Folding III

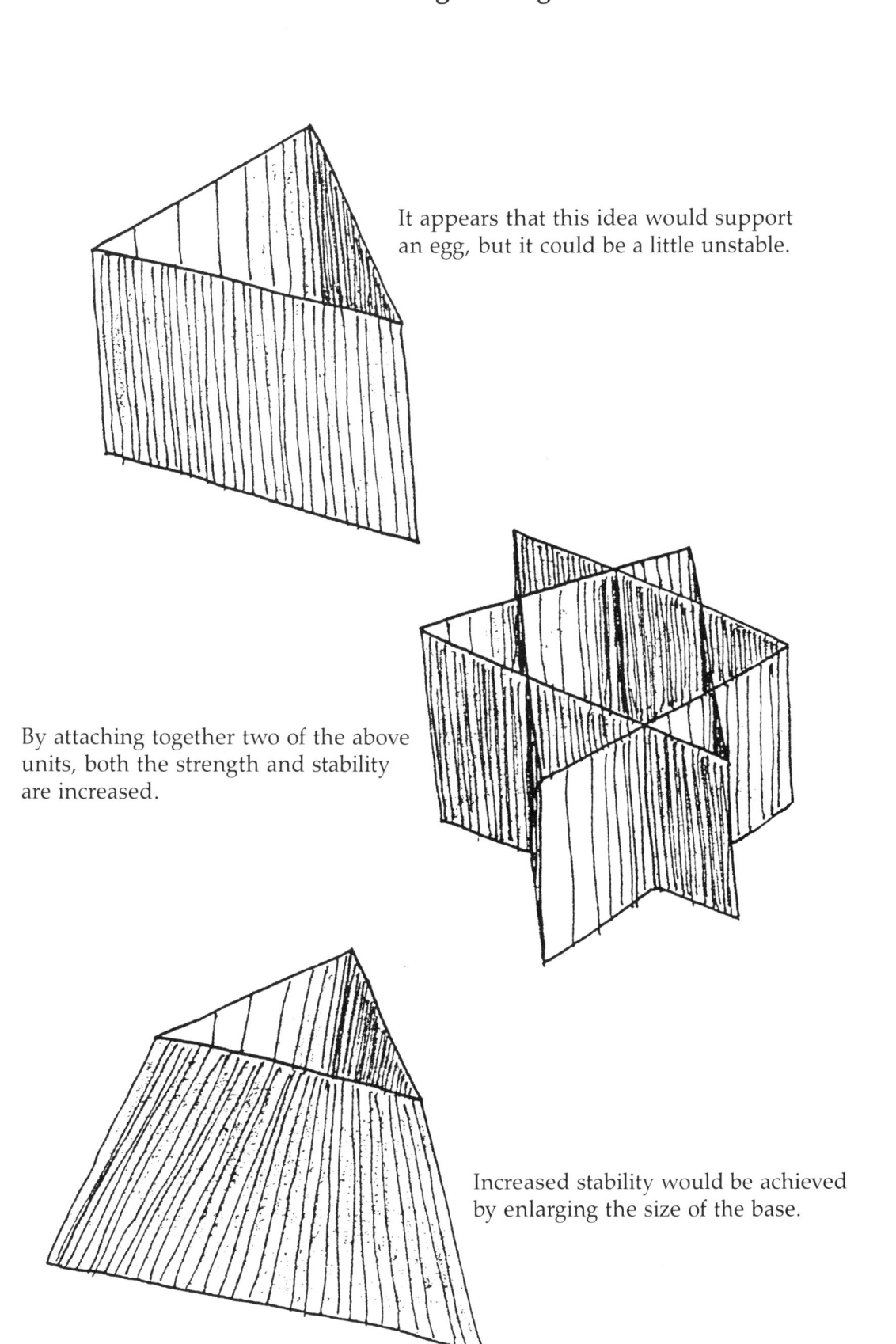

It appears that this idea would support an egg, but it could be a little unstable.

By attaching together two of the above units, both the strength and stability are increased.

Increased stability would be achieved by enlarging the size of the base.

Ideas Using Folding IV

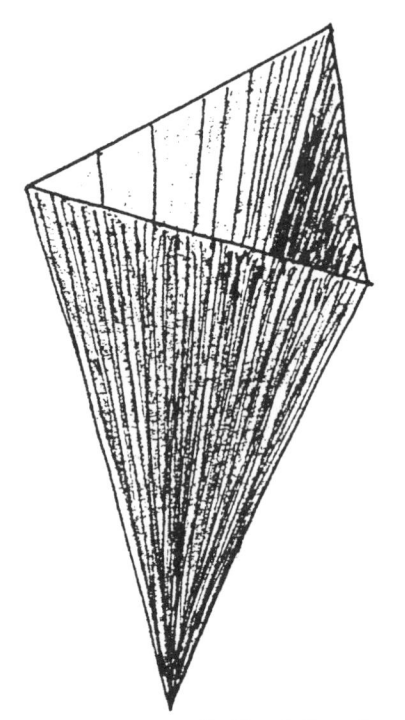

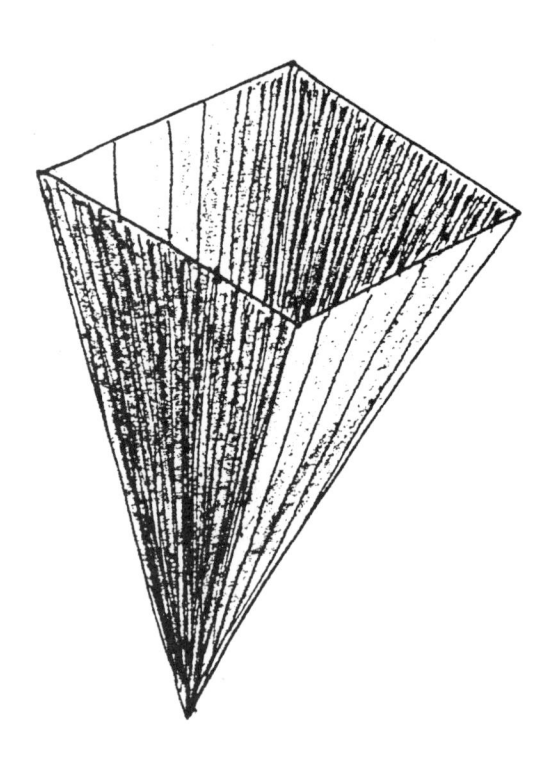

Both of the above cones would support an egg, but it could be inconvenient to have one of your hands fully occupied in holding the support.

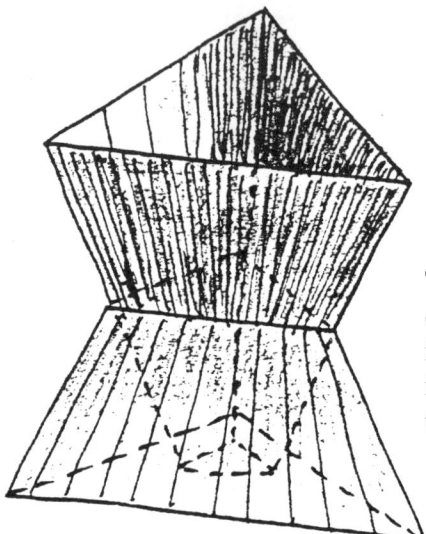

The removal of the tops of the cones, one more so than the other, and then inverting the taller cone and placing it inside the other one, would overcome the above-mentioned problem.

Ideas Using Folding V

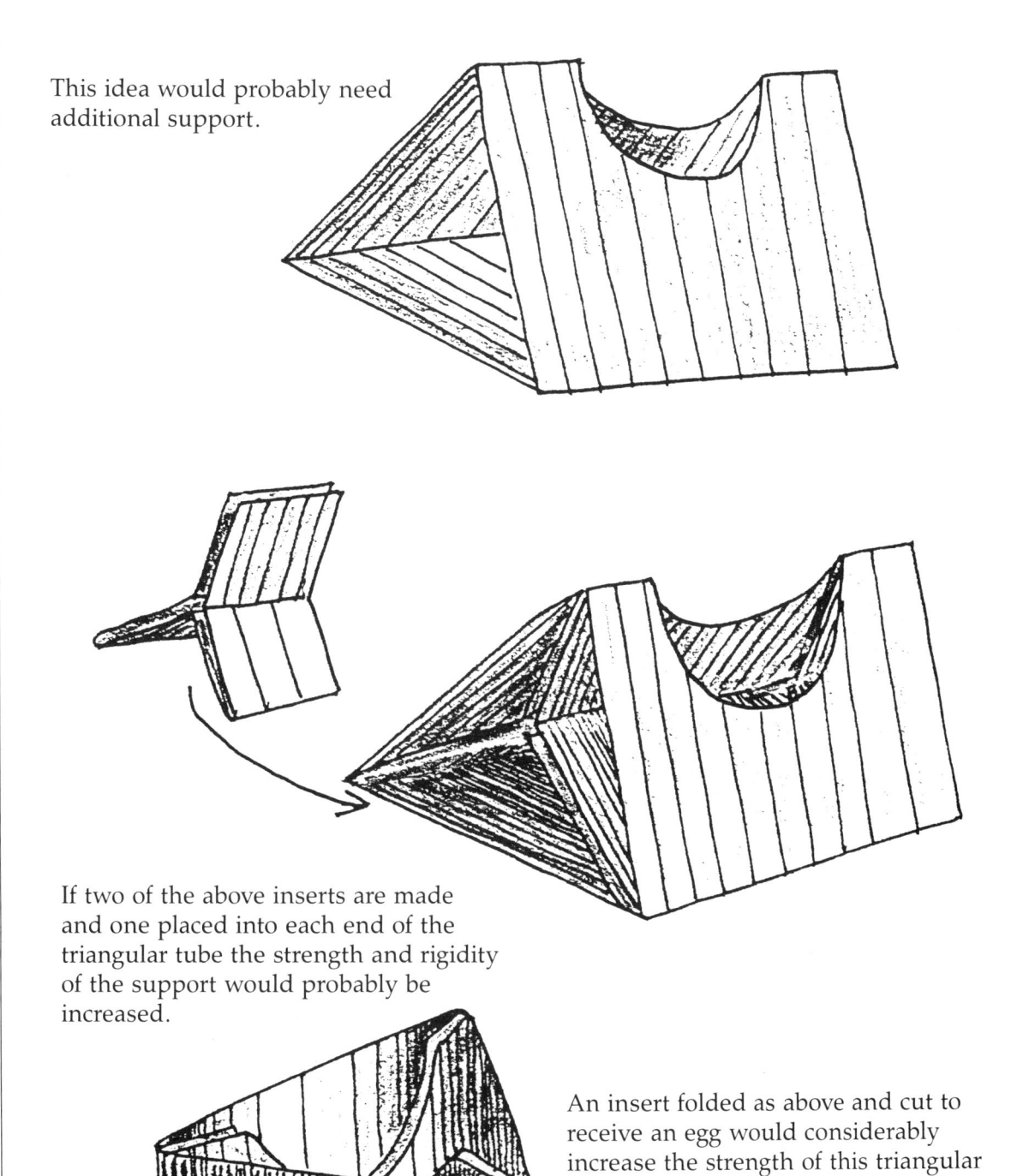

This idea would probably need additional support.

If two of the above inserts are made and one placed into each end of the triangular tube the strength and rigidity of the support would probably be increased.

An insert folded as above and cut to receive an egg would considerably increase the strength of this triangular tube.

Ideas Using Folding and Flat Pieces

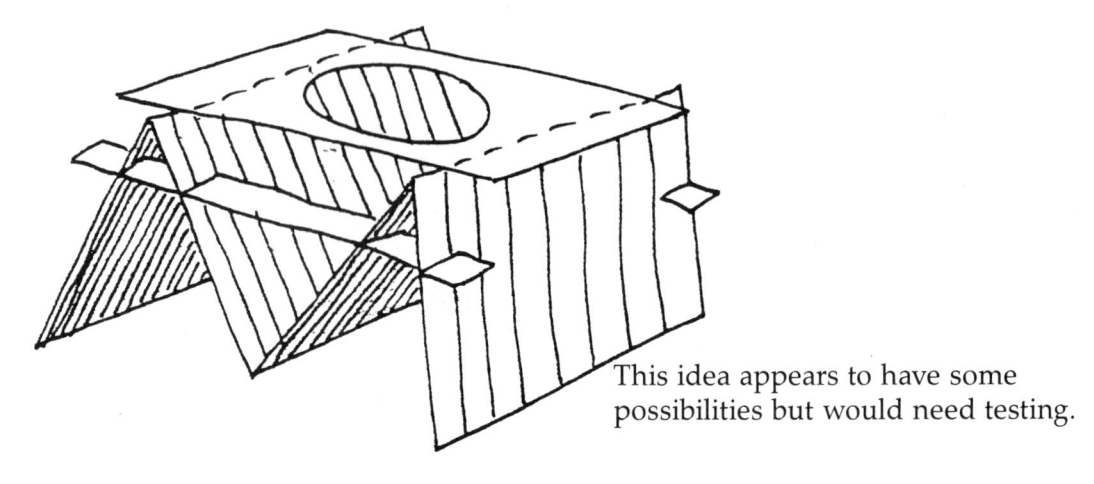

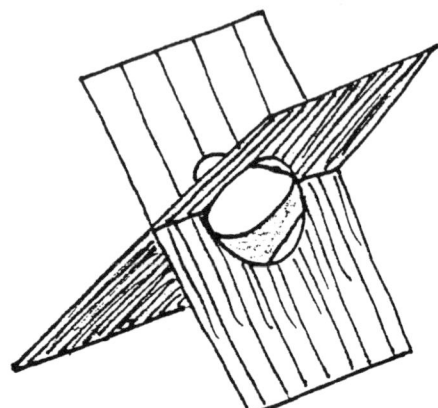

This idea appears to have some possibilities but would need testing.

The above idea in its present form would probably be too weak to support an egg.

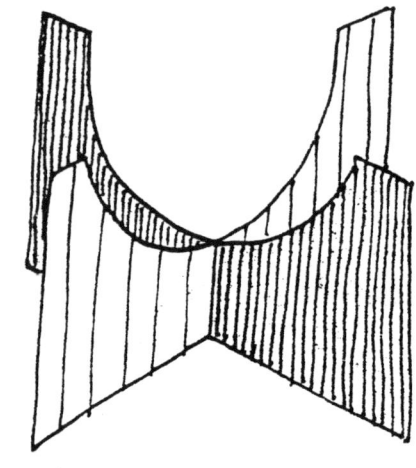

The edges of the card would probably support the weight of an egg but would probably flex around too easily.

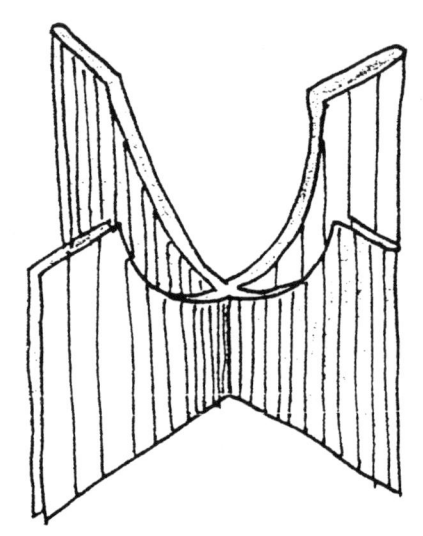

Folding the card as above would increase the strength and rigidity of the card but still might need supporting.

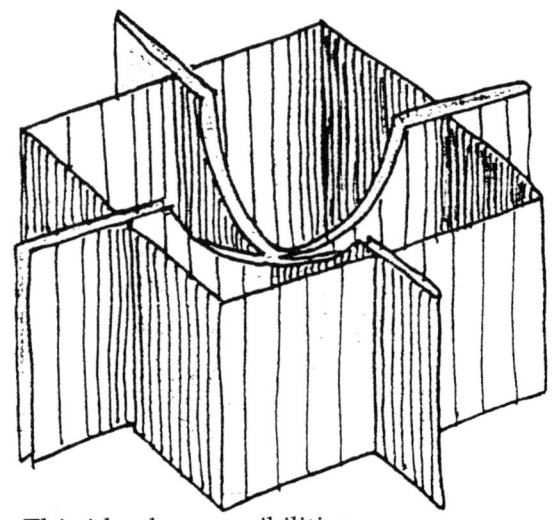

This idea has possibilities.

Ideas Using Bending and Rolling I

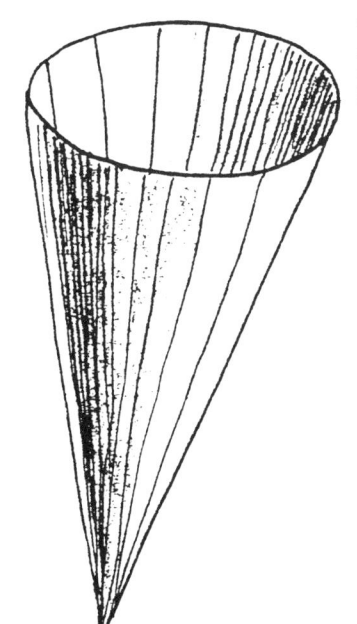

The cone would probably need to be held in one hand and therefore could be inconvenient.

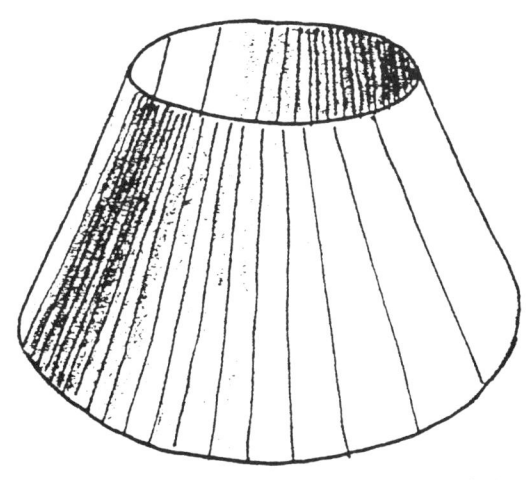

The removal of the pointed end of the cone and inverting it into the above position would produce a fairly stable support.

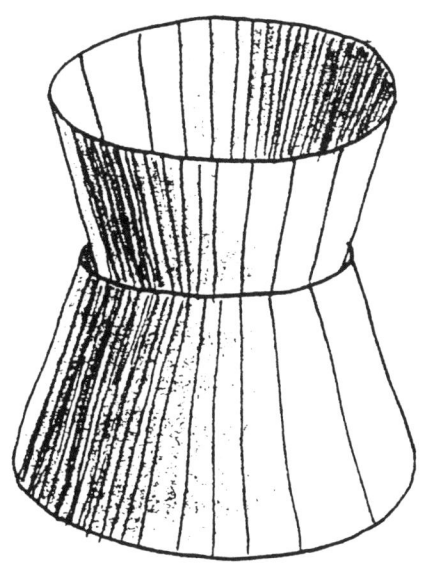

The inverted cone could also be used to support the first shape.

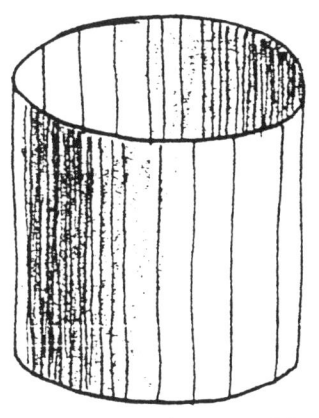

This idea would not be as stable as the inverted cone.

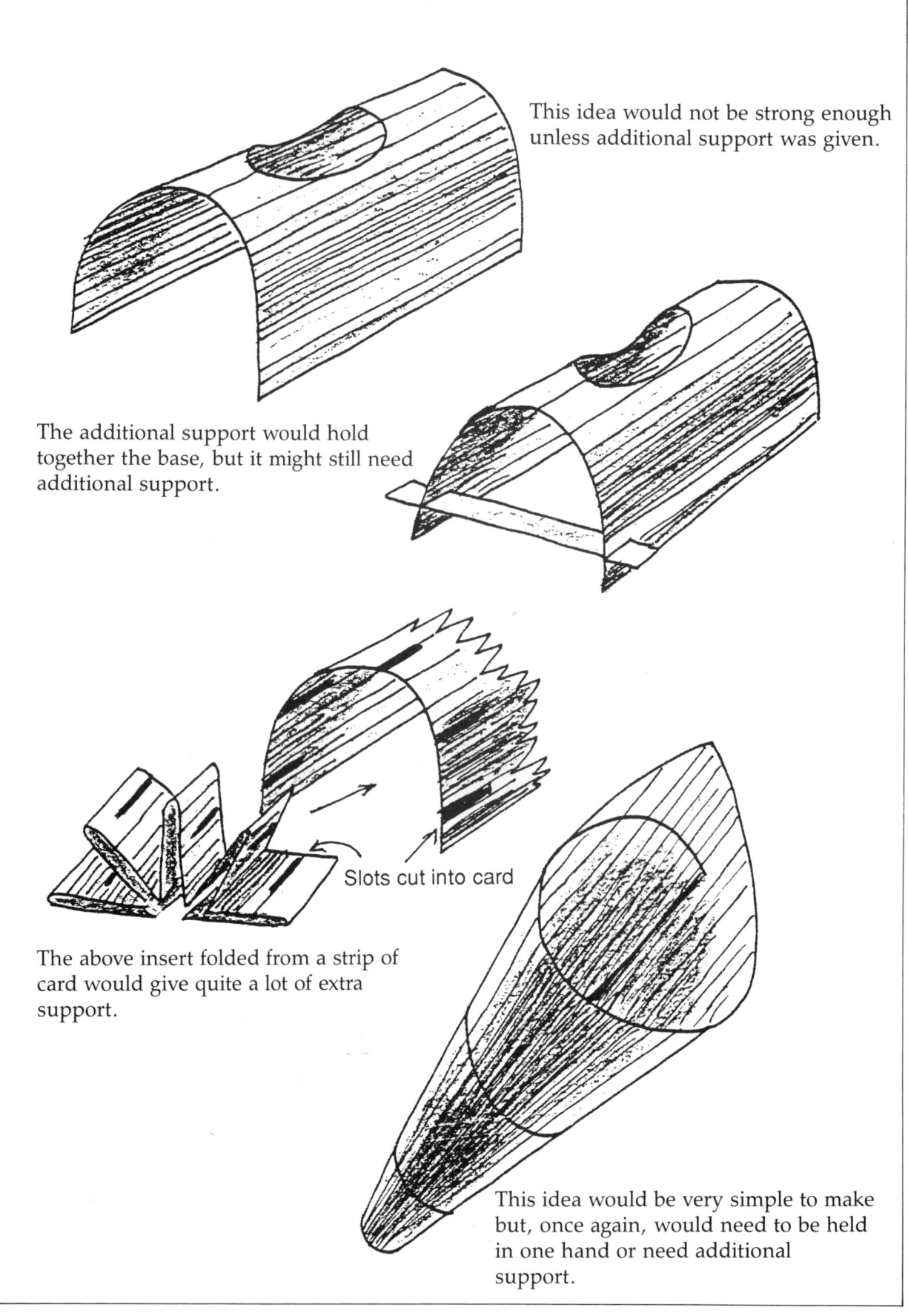

Ideas Using Bending and Rolling II

This idea would not be strong enough unless additional support was given.

The additional support would hold together the base, but it might still need additional support.

Slots cut into card

The above insert folded from a strip of card would give quite a lot of extra support.

This idea would be very simple to make but, once again, would need to be held in one hand or need additional support.

Ideas Using Bending and Rolling III

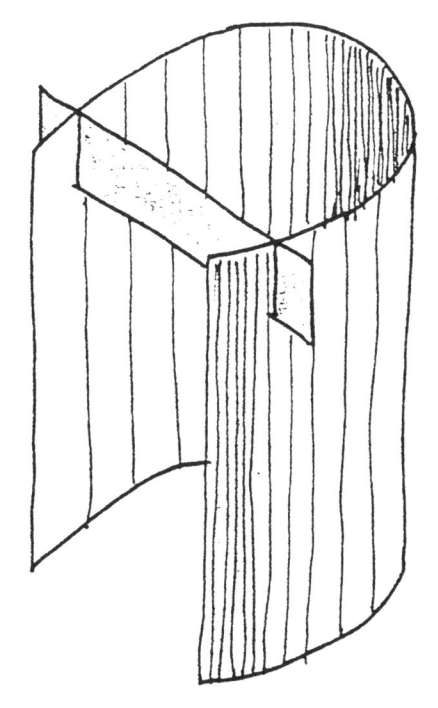

This structure appears to be very weak.

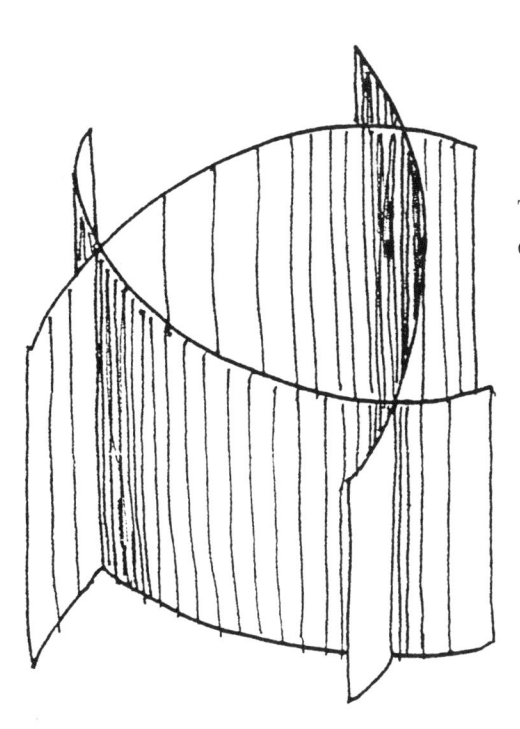

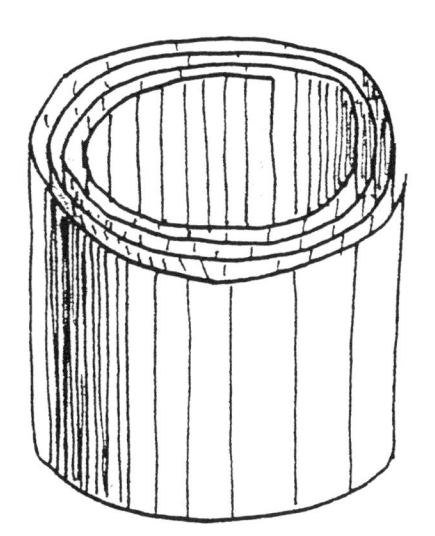

This is a very simple idea which would produce very strong walls.

The slots which need to be cut into the card would produce areas of weakness.

Ideas Combining Bending, Rolling, Folding and Flat Pieces of Card I

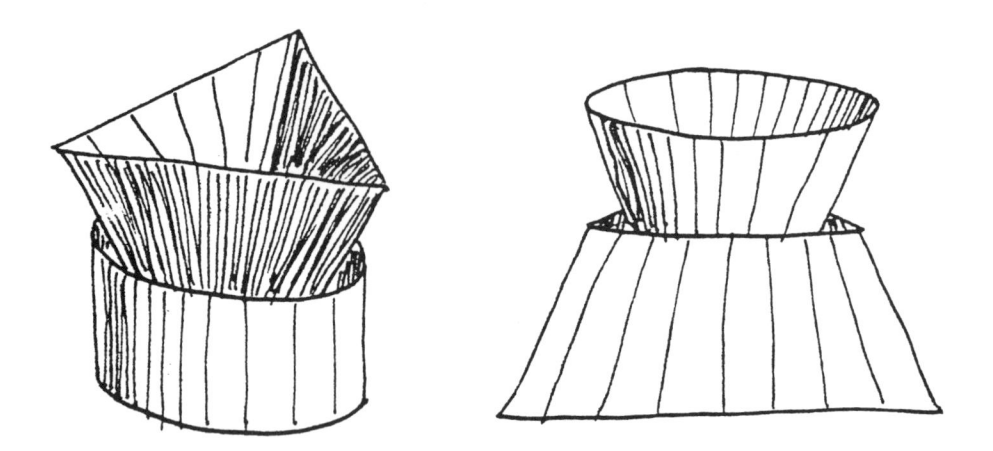

The above combinations do not appear to increase the strength of the support.

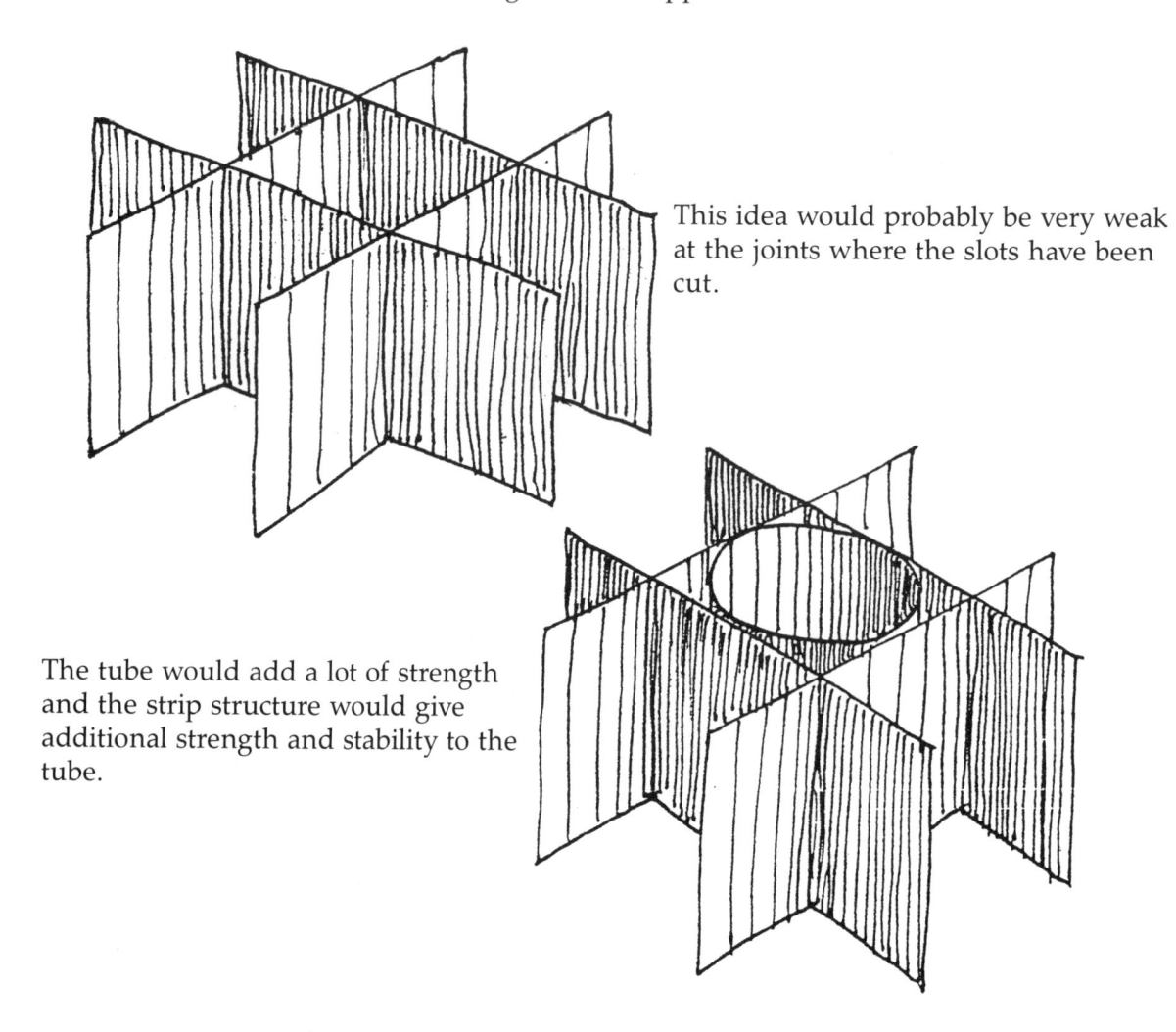

This idea would probably be very weak at the joints where the slots have been cut.

The tube would add a lot of strength and the strip structure would give additional strength and stability to the tube.

Ideas Combining Bending, Rolling, Folding and Flat Pieces of Card II

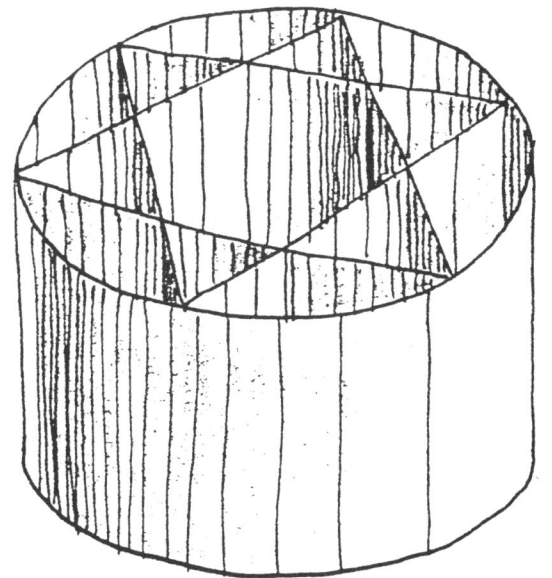

The combination of triangular and circular tubes produces a very rigid structure.

The double thickness of card forming the triangular structure makes the construction easier without loss of strength.

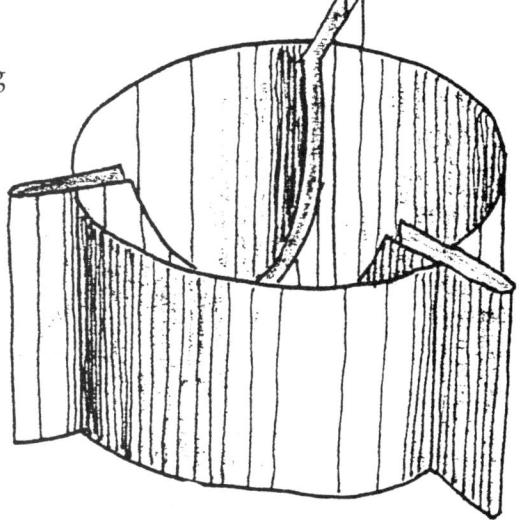

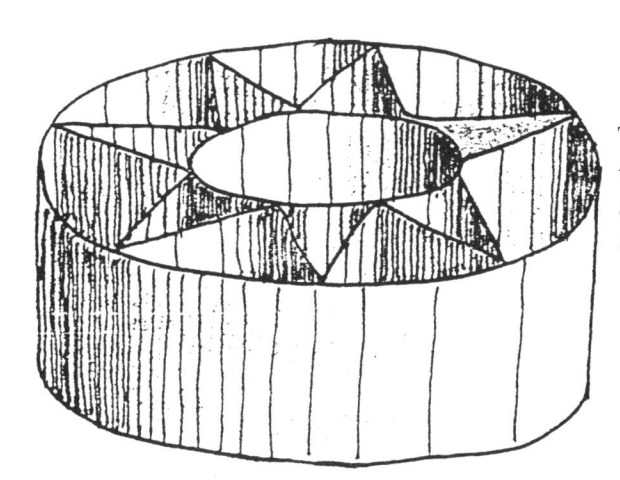

The folded strip of card inbetween the two circular tubes can easily move about and therefore may give very little additional strength to the central tube.

Development of Chosen Idea

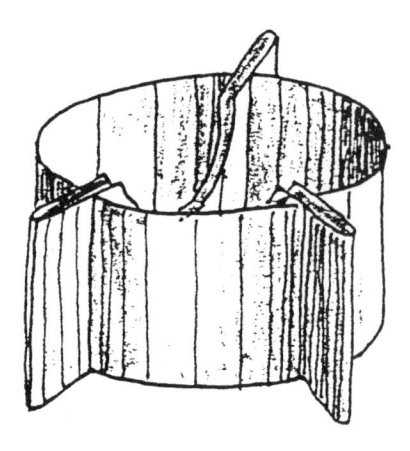

The above idea will probably support an egg but I feel that it would benefit by having additional vertical supports.

This would increase the stability of the support but would not give much contact with the egg.

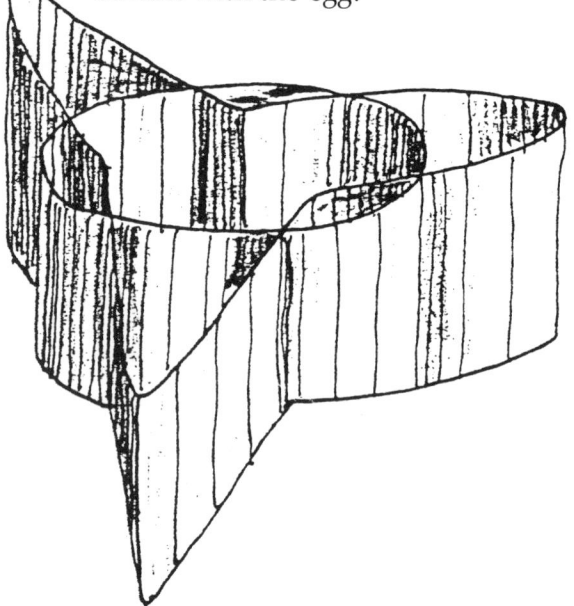

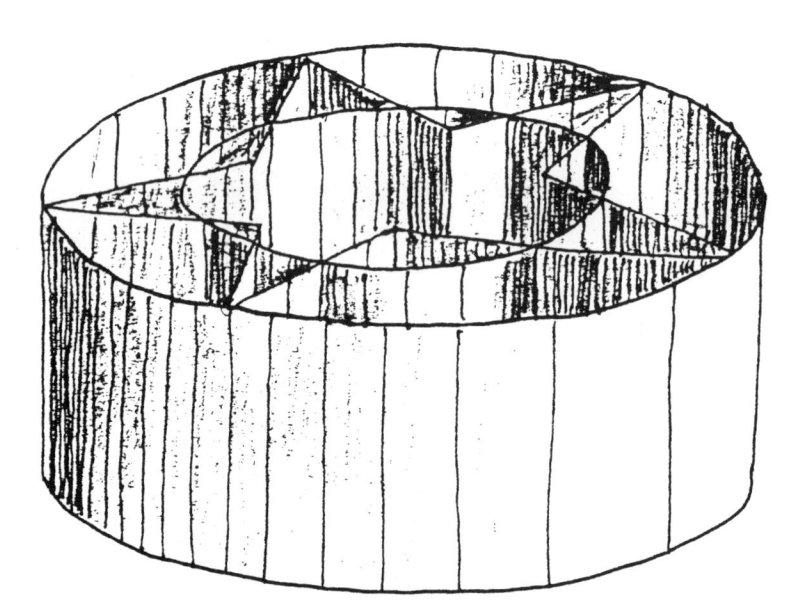

Increasing the number of triangular structures should increase the strength, and the additional tube on the outside should also add a great deal to the rigidity. The increased number of points of contact on the egg will also help to hold the egg in position.

Further Development of the Chosen Idea

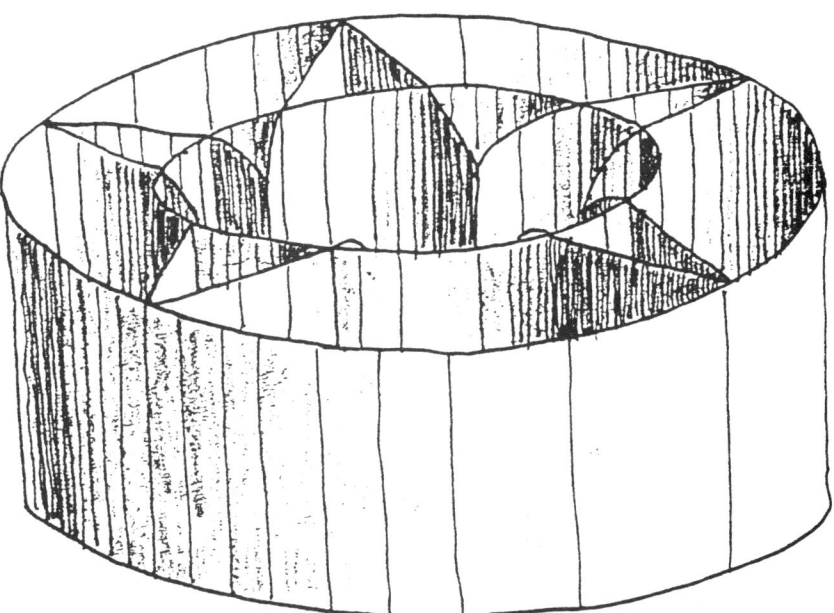

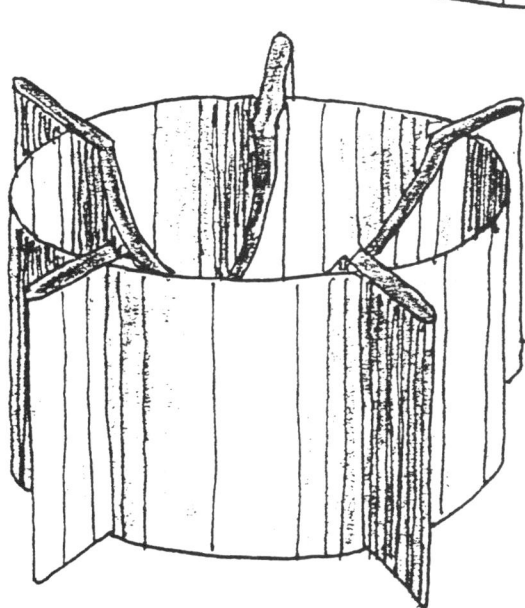

The interlocking of the folded strip into the central tube increases the strength and rigidity of the structure. If, in addition to the above, the internal triangular shapes, which contact the actual egg, are shaped to fit the shell, the area of contact will be increased and the tendency of the egg to tilt in the support will thus be reduced.

The removal of the outer tube and the extention of the vertical supports across the inner appears to maintain the strength and rigidity.

If the tubular support is reduced in height, it should still hold the five-winged vertical support in a fairly rigid manner. The slots which will have to be cut into both parts of the structure will be reduced in length, thus minimising the weakening effect on the central support.

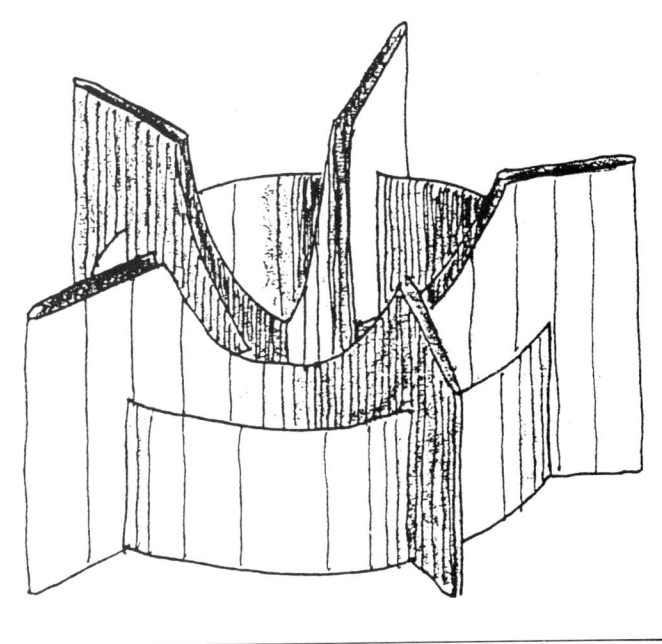

Fastening the Card

These are various techniques which could be used to fasten the card without the aid of glue, adhesive tape, paper fasteners etc.

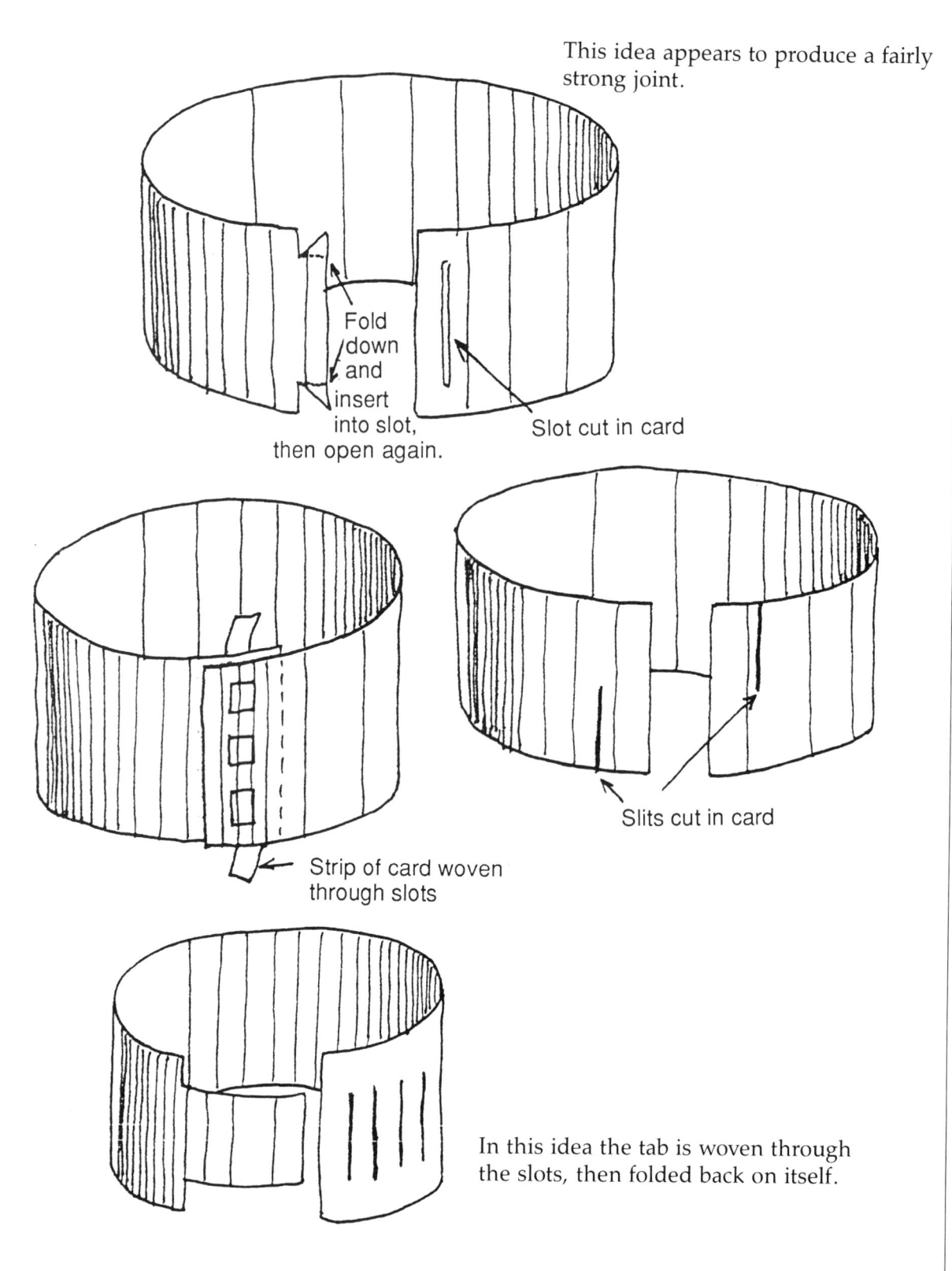

This idea appears to produce a fairly strong joint.

Fold down and insert into slot, then open again.

Slot cut in card

Strip of card woven through slots

Slits cut in card

In this idea the tab is woven through the slots, then folded back on itself.

Chosen Methods of Assembly

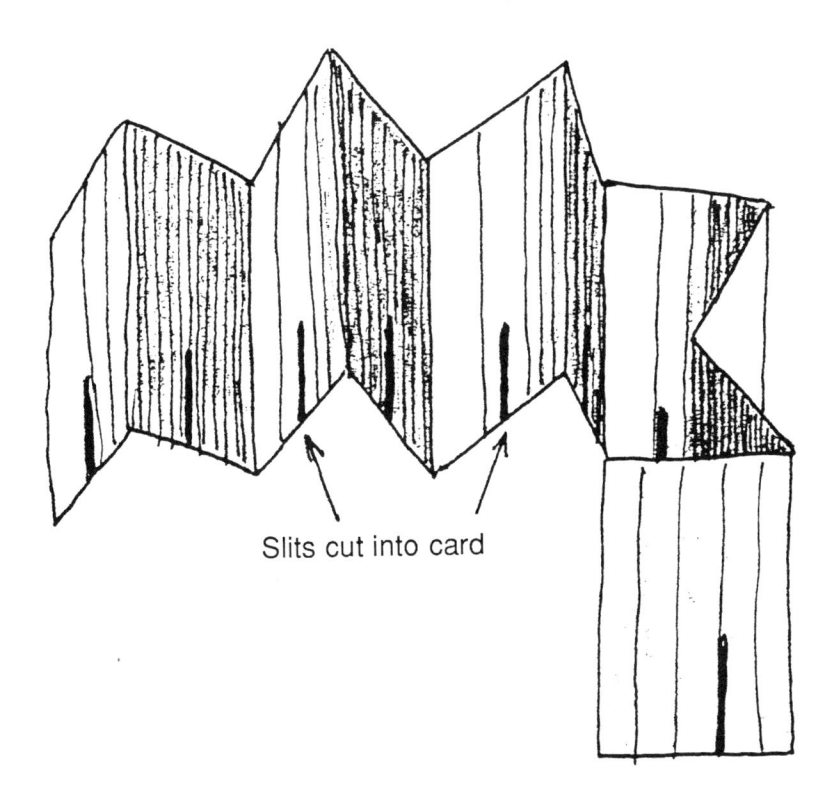

Slits cut into card

Slits cut into the card
to receive the above structure

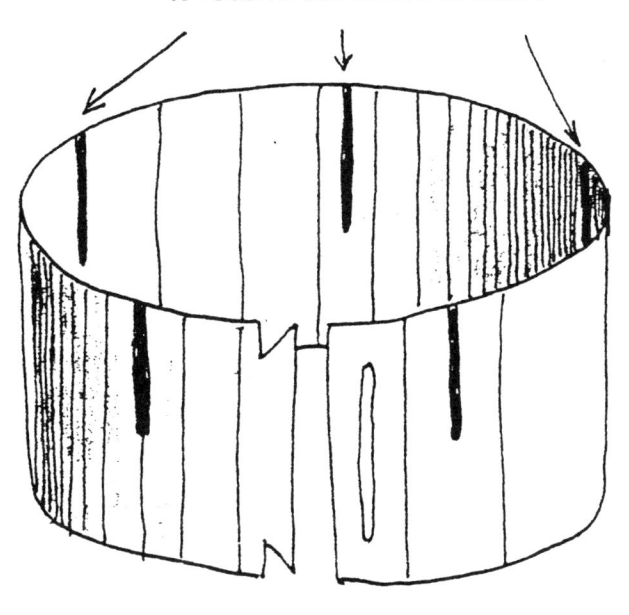

Working Drawing

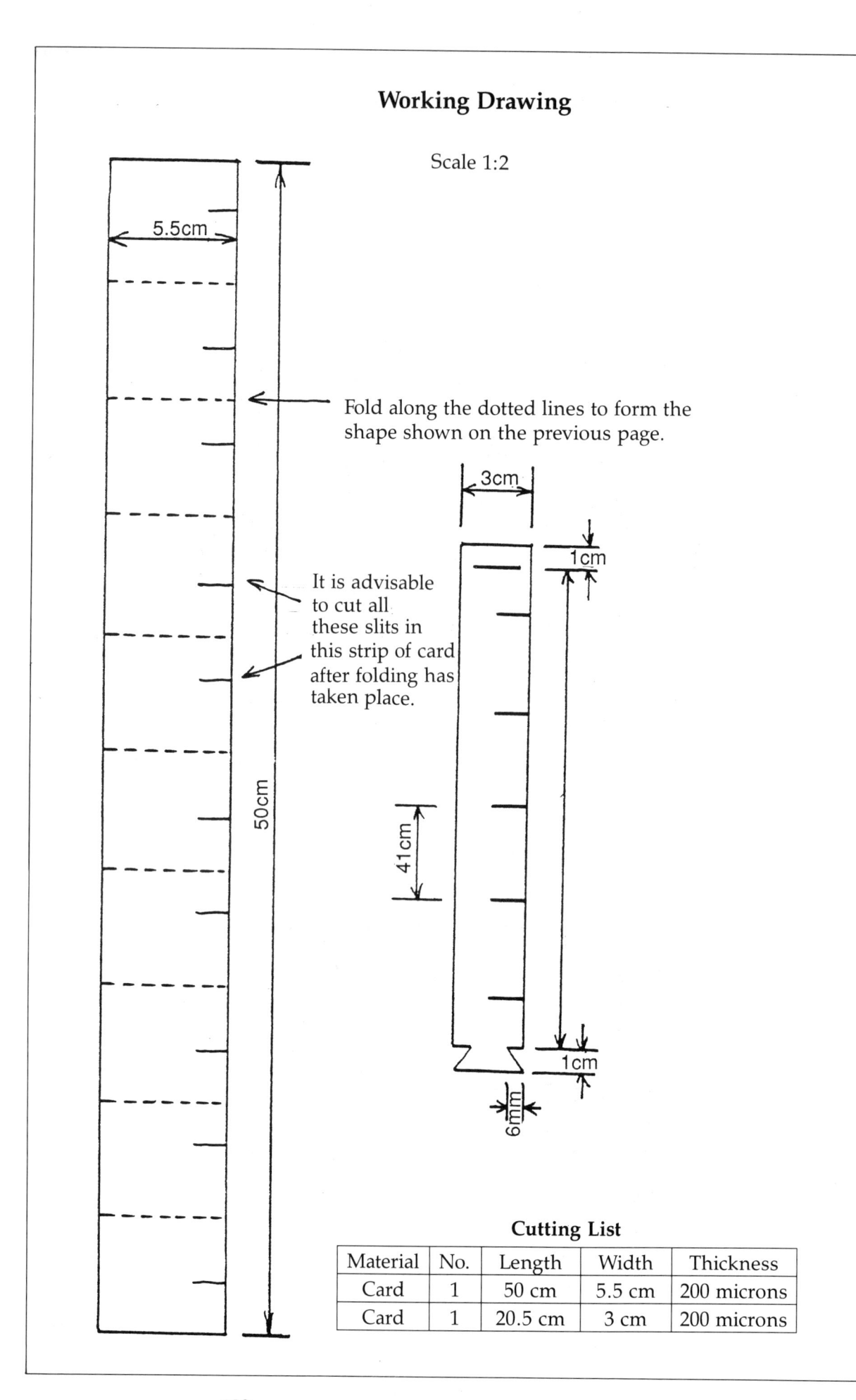

Scale 1:2

5.5cm

Fold along the dotted lines to form the shape shown on the previous page.

3cm

1cm

It is advisable to cut all these slits in this strip of card after folding has taken place.

50cm

41cm

1cm

6mm

Cutting List

Material	No.	Length	Width	Thickness
Card	1	50 cm	5.5 cm	200 microns
Card	1	20.5 cm	3 cm	200 microns

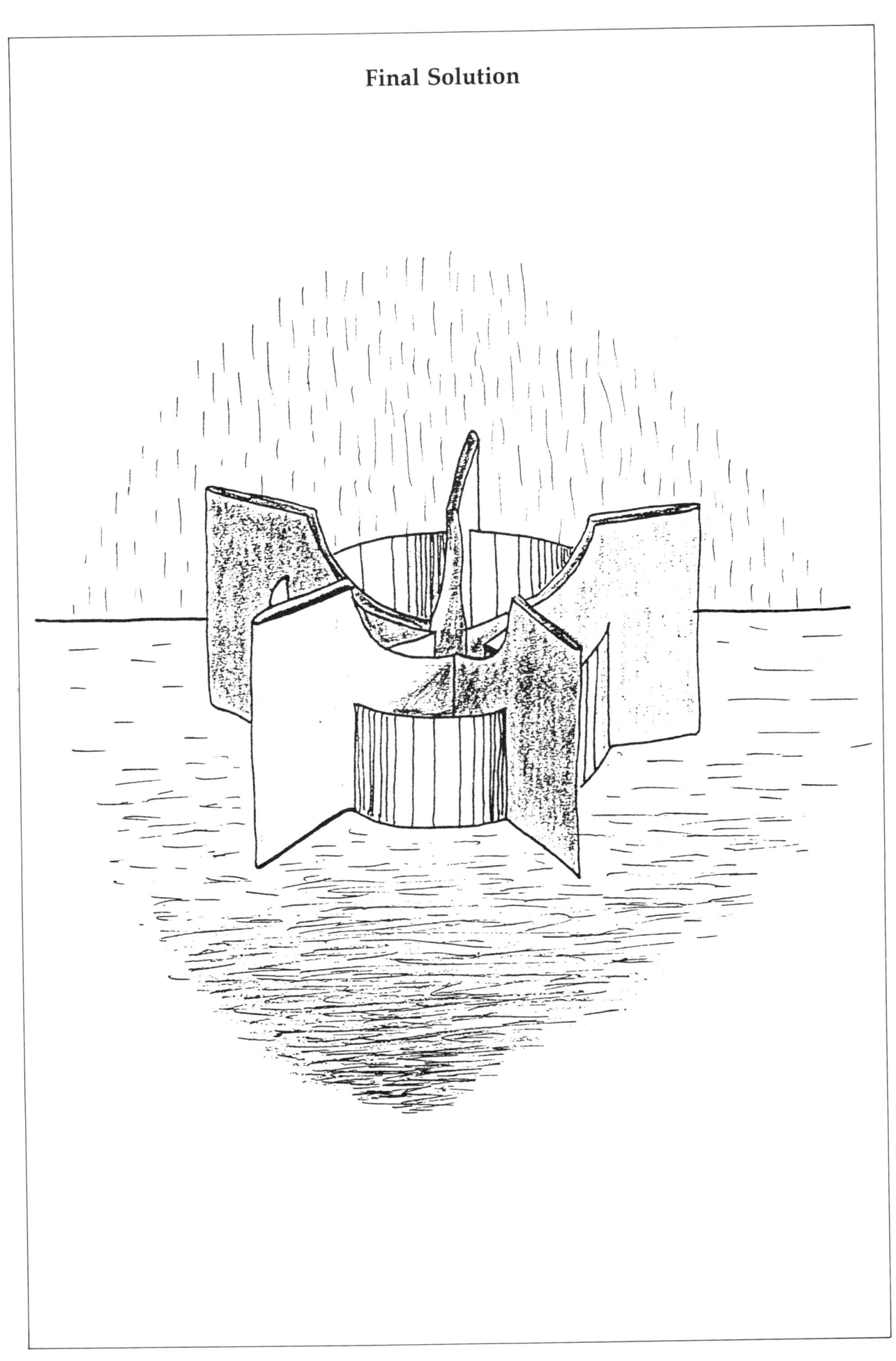

Final Solution

Evaluation

Both of the ideas shown in the photographs produced very strong egg supports; however, my final solution was the easier to make of the two. It also used less card and provided more than adequate support. In fact, the prototype, which was made out of cartridge paper, was strong enough to support a large egg without any difficulty.

If one intended to keep the support or even market the idea as a disposable egg cup, decoration could be considered in the form of different coloured card combinations, superficial coatings or even punching out shapes or embossing.

I have found the solution to be both serviceable and aesthetically pleasing and feel that further development at this stage is unnecessary.

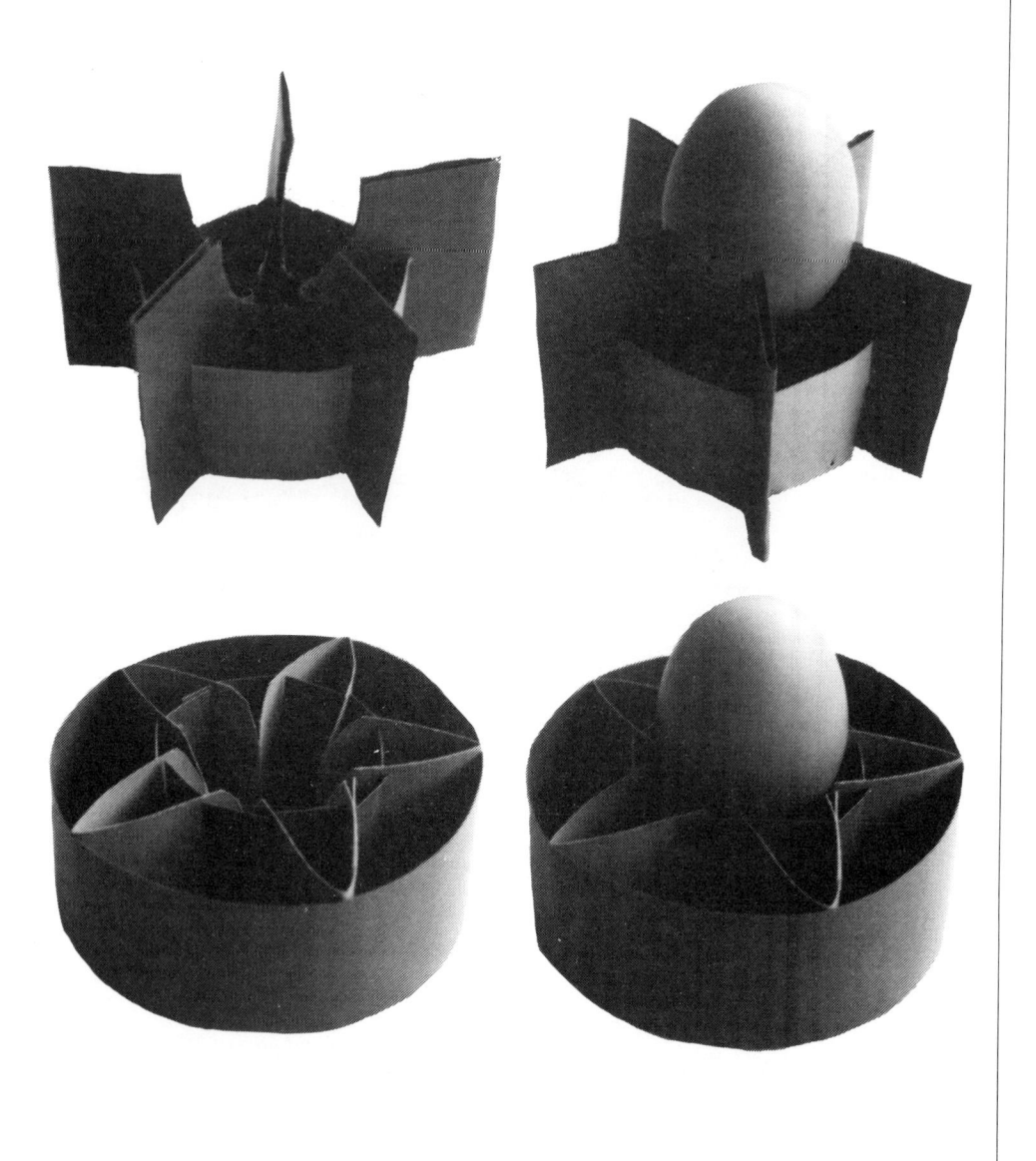

DESIGN AND PROBLEM BANK

1. Imagine that you have a 5-year-old brother/sister and are concerned because most other children of the same age appear to be able to count much better than he or she. You would like to do something to help.

2. An old lady has difficulty walking and has to use a walking stick to help her.

   This poses a problem, because when the old lady has cooked her meal in the kitchen she has great difficulty taking it through to eat in the dining room.

3. A multi-national group of 15-year-old children are visiting and want to wander around the school on their own.

   The problem is that they will not know how to find their way around the school or know which subjects are being taught in different areas.

4. You have bought an oval, glass-topped table and you are concerned that the cutlery and crockery will scratch the surface when you use it.

5. You would like to make a collection of flowers for a project that you are working on at school. Unfortunately it has to be handed in at the beginning of December when there are few flowers about. The date is now August 1st.

6. You are tackling a project where it is necessary to demonstrate the power of the wind to a group of sceptics.

7. You would like to power a small light and a transistor radio in your cottage which is situated on a remote hillside without mains supplies of water or electricity. Fresh water is obtained from a fast-flowing stream which runs by the side of the cottage.

8. Your school is going to have an open day and you want it to be well attended.

   The area where the school is situated does not allow you to display posters outside.

9. You work in a camping store and your customers are multi-national. They are constantly asking you to help them understand the workings of a butane gas stove, and how to use it safely.

   The instructions inside the box are written in English only, and you are usually so busy that you cannot spare the time to keep demonstrating how to use it.

10. A group of four girls or boys have decided to spend a week together away from home during the next week's holiday from school. By that time each will have managed to save up £15.

    You are one of the members of the above group and you have been asked to plan the trip.

11. Imagine that you are going into hospital for a few weeks. You will be leaving at home one adult and two children to look after themselves.

    The problem is that you need to produce seven main meals on a budget of £10 a week, with nutritional value your main concern, and no member of the family can read. The adult remaining at home does not usually prepare any meals, and the two children are both 7 years old.

12. I like to go away for a week at a time on a cycling or camping holiday. Unfortunately, I have difficulty carrying all the food and equipment.

13. A disabled person is confined to a wheelchair and has difficulty picking up small objects which have fallen on the floor. You would like to help him in some way.

14. A confectioner is concerned about preventing items, bought from his shop, being damaged in transit to the customers' homes, especially when they are bought in numbers of four or more.

15. A middle school teacher grows very frustrated at the number of shoe laces she has to tie each day, because the children either do not know how to fasten them, or they have forgotten how.

16. You like to go to bed quite early. Your neighbour's son plays his record player at an acceptable level under normal circumstances but the bedroom walls are made of plasterboard and allow the sound to pass straight through. This, of course, prevents you from going to sleep.

17. Above the coal fire is a 5 ft long by 6 in wide bare wooden shelf, and above that is a featureless wall.

    You would like to make the area look more interesting.

18. Two brothers or sisters sleep in the same room. One of them likes to read in bed, whilst the other one likes to go straight to sleep.

    The only light source is the central light bulb, and this causes obvious problems.

19. You like to go into the Dales for long hikes, especially in winter. One of your main concerns is heat loss from the body. You have managed to overcome this problem to some extent, except for the neck and head region.

20. One of your friends invited you to a party and you wore your one and only outfit. You have now been invited to another party in three weeks' time and the same people will be there. You have no money or any chance of obtaining enough money to buy any new clothes. The only materials available to you are scraps up to 30 cm square and standard needlework equipment.

21. The geography department have asked your class to make a study over the next 12 months, of the local weather conditions.

    There is no apparatus in school to help you.

22. You only have time to go shopping on a Thursday or Friday night when it is late-night opening at the supermarket. This means that you have to carry all the week's shopping at one go. Consequently, you try and pack as much shopping as possible into the smallest number of bags to carry home on the bus.

    Unfortunately, modern shopping bags, even the expensive ones, are not made to last and the handles and straps on them are always letting you down by breaking under the great strain put upon them. The plastic carriers, sold at the supermarket, are not made to withstand heavy loads over a long distance.

23. You are going on a trip to France, for the third time, and although you do not speak any French, you find that there are very few words and phrases you need to use. Unfortunately, it takes such a long time to find the translations, wading through lots of apparently useless information, which must be very frustrating for the French person with whom you are trying to communicate.

24. When writing an essay for school or a letter to one of your friends, you constantly repeat yourself and find that you have written about the wrong thing in the wrong place on the same letter.

25. From a map, select an unpopulated area and choose an interesting campsite. Your objective is to camp as near as possible to the widest range of land formations available in one area.

    Three other people will be accompanying you, and they would like to see the exact shape of these formations viewed from the campsite and what they are called, so that they can judge for themselves if the area is worth visiting.

    Disregard any other land formations which may block out the view of any of those being observed.

26. Imagine that you are the caretaker, and the Headmaster is frequently complaining to you about the amount of litter in and around the school.

27. The school paid for a trip that you went on when you could not afford to go. The school is now in slight financial difficulty and you feel that you would like to do something about it.

28. The Headmaster asked all the pupils in school to fill in a questionnaire, and he has found out that about half of the pupils think that there should be some kind of school uniform, and find the present one acceptable. The other half do not like it.

    The Headmaster would like to have a large majority of the pupils supporting the choice of clothing worn for school.

29. It is very close to Christmas and the shops have sold out of ready-made decorations. You would like to decorate your living room.

30. You live out in the country in an expensive house with a very long drive. The drive passes over a paddock containing 5 horses.

    The gate at the exit is set back from a narrow country road to allow room for visitors in cars to pull in, out of danger of any passing traffic, whilst someone opens the gate.

    A tall hedge borders each side of the road.

    The problem is that people bring bags of rubbish, old washing machines, etc., out into the countryside to dump, and pull in at the entrance to your house, because it appears to be a convenient dumping area. This is because your gateway is not too far for people to travel and it is the first point along this road where a car can pull in and not be easily observed.

    Your house is also out of sight of the gate, therefore does not act as a deterrent.

31. You are in charge of a hospital and visitors to the patients bring a lot of dirt and, consequently, germs into the wards on their shoes.

    You would like to prevent this occurring, or at least reduce the problem.

32. You have bought a .177 air rifle but you find it rather boring shooting at the targets provided. You would not shoot at birds or animals but would like to make shooting more interesting.

33. You have fairly long hair and would like to keep it that way. The problem is that it is always covering your face, especially when you bend down to do anything.

34. Next year it is your parents' Silver Wedding and you and your brother/sister would like to arrange something to celebrate the occasion.

35. Your parents have given you permission to convert the spare bedroom into a bed-sitting-room for yourself.

    They have allowed you to spend up to £750.

36. Your mother is trying to lose weight but is eating too much of the wrong foods, and you would like to help her.

37. I would like to catch a pike but the type of lure the local fishing tackle shop sells has not been successful.

38. You want to put wild-bird food out for the birds in your garden but because you throw it onto the ground it has started to attract rats and mice.

39. A married couple have four sons who work away from home, but often go back home to stay for a few days, although not always at the same time.

    None of the sons can give more than one day's notice that they will be arriving and this causes the problem, for the parents, of not knowing how much milk to order until the evening of the day before the visit.

40. You want to boil an egg for three minutes but you always make a mistake because you can never remember the time you started, or you forget about the egg and overcook it.

41. You would like to go fishing but you have lost all of your fishing floats, and because of public holidays the shops will be closed for the next few days.

42. You would like to weigh objects of up to 2 kg but you do not want the inconvenience of having to use separate weights.

43. You have a very young baby and would like some way of keeping it entertained for short periods, when it is upstairs in its cot, so that you could do odd jobs around the house.

44. You have been given a pet rabbit (or mouse) by your friend who is moving to another country.

    The animal is at present in a cardboard box.

    Your friend has gone and cannot be contacted, when you realise that you do not have anything to keep it in and the animal will soon escape from the cardboard box.

    Another difficulty is that the shops are closed for the next four days because of holidays.

45. You would like to breed successfully, live-bearing tropical fish, e.g. guppies. However, they always eat their own young and you have had little success with breeding traps that you have bought.

46. You are a member of a youth club which has a membership of approximately 100. Members are always complaining that there is never anything to do except the normal activities available, such as music, table tennis, pool etc.

    You would like to do something about it.

47. Your anxiety, at the moment, is how you are going to cope with your four guinea pigs when the weather becomes colder.

    The hutch they live in is too big to go into the house, and when the weather is cold you have to put them into cardboard boxes. These soon become soggy, however, and you do not have an unlimited number of boxes available.

48. You often leave the house to go for a training run. Unfortunately, the house is then unattended and you are concerned about leaving it unlocked.

49. You are one of a group of boys and girls who have complained that there is not enough to do during the lunch hour.

    You have been told that the gymnasium is available.

50. The person in charge of the 5th year leavers' party has been taken ill, before having time to arrange anything, and you would like to have a party.

51. You have been told by your teacher that the heat produced by a lighted candle can generate enough power to move things; however, he did not give any examples and you would like to convince your friends about this concept but you are finding it very difficult.

52. You have recently moved house and the front garden is in a very run-down state. The garden is 10 yds by 15 yds and is flat. You are worried what the neighbours might think of you if something is not done about it fairly quickly but you can only afford to spend up to £250 on it.

53. Your room faces south thus creating the problem of the sunlight fading the furnishings.

54. You have been invited to a fancy dress party where the theme is insects and bugs.

DESIGN BRIEFS

1. A local fashion designer is going to exhibit his work at your school and you have offered to help to give the event maximum publicity.

2. Your school is organising a fair based upon an international theme. It is to take place in the main hall and you need to produce ideas for suitable decorations.

3. You are on a committee which has to put forward recommendations for the design of an ocean-going research vessel. Each member of the committee must produce his own design for the vessel as a starting point for discussions with the shipbuilders.

4. Produce an advertising campaign selling the idea of a holiday in West Yorkshire to a group of Americans. Assume that they know very little about the area.

5. You have inherited an antique shawl which you want to make into a decorative feature in your living room. It is a 1920s, art deco, silk and gold shawl, heavily decorated with a dragon motif.

6. The school has acquired an exhibition of the growth of Industrial Bradford during the early 19th century and you have been asked to design the room-setting for this and a decorative cover for the information booklet.

Bibliography

de Bono, E., *The Use of Lateral Thinking,* Jonathan Cape Ltd., 1967.

de Bono, E., *Lateral Thinking,* Ward Lock Educational, 1970.

de Bono, E., *CoRT Thinking – Teacher Notes I-V,* Direct Education Services Ltd., 1975.

de Bono, E., *Thinking Action – Teachers' Handbook – CoRT VI,* Direct Services Ltd., 1976.

de Bono, E., *The Happiness Purpose,* Temple Smith, 1977.

Kahney, H., *Problem Solving – A Cognitive Approach,* Open University, 1986.

Jackson, K. F., *The Art of Solving Problems,* The Bulmershe-Comino Problem-solving project at Bulmershe College, Reading, Berks, 1983.

Jones, J. C., *Designing Methods,* John Wiley and Sons Ltd., 1970.

Schools Council Modular Courses in Technology – Problem Solving, Oliver and Boyd, 1972.